JAYS!

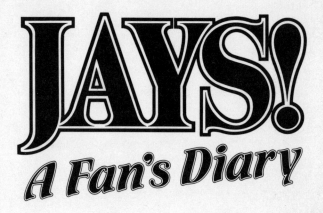

JAYS!
A Fan's Diary

Jon Caulfield

McClelland and Stewart

McClelland and Stewart Limited
The Canadian Publishers
25 Hollinger Road, Toronto M4B 3G2

Canadian Cataloguing in Publication Data

Caulfield, Jon.
    Jays! : a fan's diary

ISBN 0-7710-1931-9

1. Toronto Blue Jays (Baseball team).
I. Title.

GV875.T6C38 1985   796.357'64'09713541   C85-098268-5

Printed and bound in Canada

Contents

For Dick Smith,
who taught me how to keep a scorecard.

This book is about a baseball team and about the game itself—the game between the lines.

If you stay with this game and really watch it, your appreciation goes much deeper. It rewards you.
— Ted Simmons

More than any other sport, baseball creates the magnetic, addictive illusion that it can almost be understood.
— Tom Boswell

ONE

Warm-Ups

Can't anyone here play this game?
— Casey Stengel

If you ain't got a bullpen, you ain't got nothin'.
— Yogi Berra

February 16

The Toronto Blue Jays' first seven seasons were bunched in two clumps. During the first clump, which lasted five years, they did not play so hot, and when those five years were over, they had registered a record for futility exceeded among expansion clubs by only the incomparable New York Mets. And no expansion club, even the Mets, had a worse fifth season than the Jays. The 1966 Mets had a winning percentage of .410; the 1981 Jays played .349 ball.

There were a lot of long afternoons and long nights for the Jays those first years. Expansion baseball means maulings. It means too many enemy batsmen given passes to first, too many pegs gone in dugouts, too many third strikes blankly looked at. It means starters rocked in the first – and games for all practical purposes over nearly before they have begun – and relievers rocked at will. It means balls dropping in and squibbing through which want to be caught. And it means too, too few runs. The Jays scored the hard way those early days. Base-hit, base-hit, base-hit, base-hit. Yield: one run, three left-on-base.

They were not years wholly without moments when it seemed maybe the Jays *could* play this game: Jesse Jefferson finding his concentration and the corners one summer afternoon and mowing down Twins in sudden bunches; Otto Velez blowing out the Tribe with a violent outburst of longball; Jerry Garvin nailing a Bosock base runner with a pickoff move like a snake's pounce; Roy Howell and John Mayberry turning a nifty five-three-five double play to snuff a Brewer rally. There were the season Bob Bailor hit .310, the day Howell drove in nine runs, Dave Lemanczyk's thirteen dogged wins that first hard summer. (Bailor, .310; Howell, nine; Lemanczyk, thirteen – numbers and more numbers. R.b.i's and e.r.a.'s. HR's, K's, and sac.'s. A.b.'s, b.b.'s, 3b's, and l.o.b.'s. D.p.'s, i.p.'s, and w.p.'s. Baseball is reckoned in numbers. No other sport keeps so exhaustive an arithmetic, in part because no other sport is so reducible to measurable fragments. To the non-fan the numbers are gibberish, and the fan's preoccupation with decimals and

2

ordinals and cardinals seems a compulsion. But the fan is concerned not with numbers themselves but their meaning; the numbers are just symbols. The fan knows how hard it is to pitch thirteen winning ball games for an expansion club in its first season – a number matched only once and never exceeded – and the numbers after the name Lemanczyk, W 13, L 16, are more than just stats. They are a clue about why anyone bothers to care about this implausible game – try explaining it to someone wholly unfamiliar with it – at all.)

But the agreeable memories are outnumbered by others less sanguine of Jay fortunes gone awry in myriad ways. When the hitters hit, the pitchers did not pitch; when the pitchers pitched, the fielders did not field; when the hitters hit, pitchers pitched, and fielders fielded, they often seemed able to do so for only about seven innings, at which point the machine went wildly haywire. The difference between a very good ballclub and a very bad ballclub is one game in three; they will split the other two. Time and time again for the Jays those crucial third games slipped away.

The clubhouse was often a quiet place. Half-dressed ballplayers slumped on benches by their lockers and stared at spots on the floor; major league ballplayers, even lowly ones, *hate* to lose. The first manager, Roy Hartsfield, sat in his office and stared at a bottle of beer and a Bible on his desk as if maybe they offered some clue about how to stop losing. Reporters, pencils poised at notebooks, spoke in low tones like mourners at a wake, asked questions to which there were no answers except maybe one: expansion baseball. The hard numbers after five years:

Expansion Club Records After Five Seasons

	W	L	PCT.	GB
Los Angeles/California Angels (1961-65)	383	425	.474	—
Kansas City Royals (1969-73)	367	424	.464	8½

	W	L	PCT.	GB
Seattle Pilots/Milwaukee Brewers (1969-73)	353	450	.440	27½
Montreal Expos (1969-73)	345	458	.430	35½
Houston Colt 45s/Astros (1962-66)	333	475	.412	50
Seattle Mariners (1977-81)	290	465	.384	66½
Washington Senators/Texas Rangers (1961-65)	309	499	.382	74
San Diego Padres (1969-73)	294	506	.367	85
Toronto Blue Jays (1977-81)	270	482	.359	85
*New York Mets (1962-66)	260	547	.322	122

Fans and press were indulgent at first. Expansion clubs are not expected to win. But they are expected to get better, and as the seasons passed and the Jays got no better, patience turned to grumbling that grew noisier with each new string of defeats. Around the league the Jays were appraised as patsies who knew more ways to lose than anyone previously had thought up. Players on other clubs looking for new teams through free agency or trades spoke of going to Toronto the way Russian soldiers might talk about a posting to Siberia. Even worse than losing – losing when you are constantly outmatched is infuriating but unavoidable – was the utter lack of respect losing bred.

The storm's eye those years was the Jay front office, which explained its Plan for building a ballclub as often as anyone listened: a strong farm system and careful drafts and trades to acquire soundly scouted young ballplayers. No,

*The Mets' indistinction in their first half-decade was not baseball's most excessive. The 1915-19 Philadelphia Athletics played .306 ball, and their local rivals, the Phillies, played from 1938 to 1942 at an even more modest .296 clip.

no one had ever heard of them; they were kids or players who, in other organizations, had been marginal. But trust us, the front office said. The way to build a franchise is strength from inside. Short cuts like signing deluxe free agents and trading youth for established players are quick fixes which mortgage a club's future for the sake of a fly-by-night demicontender.

The betting line floated about whether this explanation was horsefeathers or good sense. The Jay brass seemed to have skills for making money and not spending very much – or not, at any rate, conspicuously. The $2 million invested yearly in the Jays' six-club farm system was less visible than the team's player payroll, which remained for several years nearly baseball's lowest; and it was hard to understand why management would make do with only a part-time batting coach for a team that could not hit. And Toronto's sports fans had been asked to swallow several seasons of indigestible flack about light at the ends of the tunnels of the city's hockey and football clubs, which bred a certain scepticism about front office promises of better days ahead.

It was, though, plain fact that expansion teams which had achieved modest early success had done so precisely by following the strategy Jay management said it had adopted. The 1969 New York Mets remain the only expansion club that has won a World Series and its pitching staff, the club's backbone, included Tom Seaver, Jerry Koosman, Nolan Ryan, and Tug McGraw. The oldest was twenty-five, all broke into the major leagues as Mets and went on to distinguished careers, and two, Seaver and Ryan, will likely enter the Hall of Fame. The Kansas City Royals' 1976 division championship was due in no small measure to the play of a twenty-three-year-old farm-grown third baseman, the league's leading hitter that year, George Brett. Dennis Leonard, another K.C. farm grad, also twenty-three, logged seventeen wins that season.

And the unhappy record of the San Diego Padres was

proof enough that dipping into the prime free agent market promised nothing. It took a lot of McDonald's burgers, the Padres' financial base, to pay the salaries of Rollie Fingers, Oscar Gamble, and Gene Tenace, and with all three yoked in San Diego's chocolate-and-lemon livery, the Padres managed a winning season barely and once, in 1978, before slumping back to their division cellar. (The Padres have not, however, suffered misgivings about recruitment of top-o'-the-line free agents. In 1983 they signed Steve Garvey, and early in 1984 they retained the services of relief pitcher Rick Gossage.* The Jays, whose relief corps left one or two things to be desired in 1983, courted Gossage too, but the Goose preferred to play ball in San Diego's warm weather.)

Jay management never claimed the Master Plan would be quick. A pennant contender, they said, was still several seasons away. As it turned out, they were nearly wrong. But for want of a bullpen, the Jays might almost have won a pennant much sooner.

February 17

In their sixth season the Jays turned sharply around. The first glimmerings of competence had occurred, in fact, in the midst of that ill-starred fifth season but were submerged by a horrible spring and autumn tailspin. There were two main reasons for the team's reversed fortunes.

One, the club hired the Jays' first real manager, Bobby Cox. Hartsfield and his successor, Bobby Mattick, had been, in effect, caretaker managers, older men without major league managerial experience who provided paternal supervision of the odds and sods of the early Jay rosters while the front office planned and built. Cox, at forty, was

---

* As San Diego has since demonstrated, careful acquisition of prime free agents may, on occasion, be a successful tactic for a struggling franchise. With Garvey and Gossage on side, a remarkably young Padre club copped the 1984 N.L. flag.

embarked on a promising managerial career; he had demonstrated an ability to shape a young team during four seasons with the Atlanta Braves. Along with Cox the club also hired its first real batting coach, Cito Gaston.

Two, the team on the field played a different kind of ball than its predecessors. It was not a different team. Only minor roster changes had been made. But the unknown kids who were the roster's bulwark were, by 1982, older and smarter and better at their jobs. A solid starting rotation finally clicked into place; Dave Stieb, Jim Clancy, and Luis Leal were the strongest front line in the majors that year. Meanwhile, the hitters, who during 1981 had been mired in a godawful slump, added under Cito Gaston's guidance nearly forty points and a run a game to the club's batting and scoring averages. The strongest offensive work was done by Damaso Garcia, acquired from the Yankees in a 1979 trade and one of the bricks the front office meant when it spoke of a foundation for the future, who batted .310, scored eighty-nine runs, and stole fifty-four bases. Afield, the Jays recorded enemy outs with new dexterity: Garcia graced second base with polish; rookie Jesse Barfield stepped into rightfield with one of the best outfield arms in the league; and shortstop Alfredo Griffin, centrefielder Lloyd Moseby, and catcher Ernie Whitt had measurably honed their defensive skills.

There were gaps. The most obvious was power. The club got dreadful performance from its designated hitter spot and trailed the league in home runs. (Home runs are not, of course, everything. The team with the fewest home runs in either league that year, the St. Louis Cardinals, also won the World Series, defeating the club which had hit the most, the Milwaukee Brewers. But the Cardinals play in spacious Busch Stadium and specialize in a distinctly National League rabbit-style of baseball. Among the lumbercompany clubs of the American League East and playing in the A.L. East's cosy parks, teams either live by the homer or die by it.) The pitching staff, after the front three, was iffy.

Fourth starter Jim Gott, twenty-two, still needed seasoning and managed only a five-and-ten record. And while relievers Roy Lee Jackson, Joey McLaughlin, and Dale Murray won twenty-four games, they also lost twenty-one and recorded only twenty-five saves among them. And too often when the big hit or big pitch or big play was required – the mark of a winning ballclub is that it rises to such occasions consistently – the Jays reverted to expansion baseball. They lost an appalling number of one-run games, and *that* is the sure mark of a losing ballclub – the blow-outs are reckoned as write-offs; it is the squeakers that matter, are those vital third games out of three.

For all that, the 1982 Jays put some noteworthy new numbers on the board. They played .481 ball. Only two expansion teams, the 1966 California Angels and 1974 Montreal Expos, had better sixth seasons; and no expansion club besides the 1969 Mets had ever turned its franchise's history around so dramatically. The Jays did remain in their division cellar but only because they played in baseball's toughest division; in the A.L. West their record that year would have been good for fourth place. And they were no longer the basement's sole tenants, now sharing the premises with Cleveland's Indians, only a scant game behind the Yankees.

February 20

Expansion clubs have a marked tendency to zigzag and, at first glance, no one would have been very surprised if the 1983 Jays had slipped from their nearly winning ways of the prior season. But, at second glance, a decline seemed less likely for a simple reason which gets at the core of winning baseball: the Jays had the ingredients that can carry a club through times when the bats are cold and through the dog days of late summer – good starting pitching and good fielding. (These are qualities so interrelated as to be of a piece. This is clearer in respect to good fielding, of obvious aid to a pitching staff, but it is no less true the other way round. Good pitchers are easier to field behind than ungood ones, in fair part because good pitchers are predictable; fielders have a better idea of what may happen in a given situation and, hence, what fielding contingencies may occur. And good pitchers throw strikes, which keeps fielders awake.) Put in other words, if you can stop the other club from blowing you out early, you are always in the game.

That as it may, most preseason prognosticators picked the Jays to again finish last with indistinction. Yes, the starting pitching did seem solid, and yes, the addition of Cliff Johnson's bat to the lineup and Dave Collins' legs to the base paths (both were acquired in trades) would bolster the club's offense. Yes, the Jays had in Griffin and Garcia a pretty good double-play combo and in Moseby, Barfield, and George Bell a young outfield which might be among the finest in the league at some uncertain future date. But for now the Jays were still mostly kids who played in the American League East, which would once more chew them up and spit them out. Maybe, just maybe, the Jays could take Cleveland, but higher hopes were out of line. The Jays were, after all . . . well, the Jays.

Not even the Jays' most partisan fans, and certainly not the Jays themselves, were wholly prepared for the way the season did turn out. For much of the summer Toronto was a bona fide, card-carrying, honest-to-god pennant contender. The club suckerpunched its rivals by abruptly adding to its reliable starting pitching and fielding an alarmingly belligerent offence. Under Cito Gaston's further guidance the 1983 Jays raised their batting average another fifteen points, their scoring average by another run a game, and their slugging average by more than fifty points. Johnson's bat – twenty-two homers – did help, but what helped even more were the young bats of Moseby and first baseman Willie Upshaw, two more fledglings who came of age and, between them, batted .310, whacked forty-five homers, drove in 185 runs, and scored 203 runs. Garcia hit .307.

Barfield slugged twenty-seven homers, as did the catching tandem, Whitt and Buck Martinez. Part-time third baseman Rance Mulliniks hit a startling thirty-four doubles in 364 at-bats and pinch-hit at a clip of .435. At season's end the Jays led the major leagues in hitting and slugging.

Meanwhile, Bobby Cox skippered the club like a master seaman. His main strength seemed to lie, as it often does with good managers, in consistently making effective use of each player on his squad. A sound corps of irregulars on the bench and a manager's use of them are often the most conspicuous differences between good clubs and so-so clubs – a case in point is the Montreal Expos, whose failure to fulfil expectations in recent seasons may in part be traced to questions of strength and disposition of bench. At times Cox's stratagems were explicable. He had determined early on, for example, to platoon Whitt and Mulliniks, who bat left, against only right-handed pitchers and did so like clockwork, to good effect. At other times his moves appeared more like hunches – the kinds of hunches that take patterns, suggesting they are more than just guesswork but are the cogitations of a capable manager.

Respect did not come right away. Players on other clubs knew the Jays could play ball. But the noise that came through from press and fans in other big league towns was that Toronto was riding an uncanny roll of luck, playing way over its head. Any day now the bubble would pop and the Jays would crash. Who had ever heard of these people? Lloyd Moseby? Willie Upshaw? Rance Mulliniks, for crying out loud? *The Sporting News* – sometimes called baseball's Bible; conversely, the Bible may be called religion's *Sporting News* – headlined an early-season article about Stieb, Clancy, and Leal, *Who are these guys?*

One step toward respect was taken July 18 when the Royals came to town, a club which in past had habitually victimized the Jays pillar to post. Along with them came the full entourage of ABC Monday Night Baseball. Someone at the network had noticed, prognoses to the contrary, the

Jays were not folding, the bubble not popping. The Jays were in first place, had been there for weeks, through the All-Star break, and were playing better ball than any club in the majors except Atlanta. Howard Cosell & Co. were dispatched to get the story. They got it.

The game wasn't much of a cliffhanger. Martinez, Johnson, Moseby, and Barry Bonnell slugged. Jim Clancy pitched nine complete innings. The final tally was Jays 8, George Brett 2. (Brett doubled in one run and homered for another. "I'm still trying to figure out some way to get him out," said Clancy afterward.) Clancy was not, however, his strongest. The K.C.s were making some contact with his stuff, and the most noteworthy job of the night was done by Alfredo Griffin, who aided his pitcher by playing the finest game of his career, conducting a clinic in the art of shortstop and turning in five extraordinary plays for the home side. Royal manager Dick Howser said after the game, "I don't think in any one game any shortstop could play better," and some seasoned fans who saw the game, who had seen Luis Aparicio and Mark Belanger in their prime, said it was maybe the finest game they had ever seen a shortstop play. (Alfredo Griffin? Who *are* these guys?)

It was all broadcast on U.S. national air. ABC announcer Al Michaels caught the gist of the proceedings nicely when he averred, "Toronto is shocking people tonight" – Michaels, one suspected, among them. By uncanny coincidence the Jays' Monday Night Baseball coming-out gala was also Game One Thousand And One in the history of the Blue Jay franchise, hence might be read as a meaningful omen. (In the Religion of Baseball, reading entrails is a form of high ritual; divination and superstition are nearly as much a part of the game as balls and bats.)

It was not until more than a month later that the wheels came off the wagon. By the last week of August the Jays were no longer in first place. After a barrage of games against the Yankees, Brewers, and Red Sox, played mostly on the road, with only one day off since late July, the Jays had fallen to fourth. But they were still only a game and a half out, a slim enough margin to make up within a couple of days if the teams ahead of them stubbed their toes. The bloom was still flush on the rose. What occurred in that final week of August, most kindly described, is that the Jay relief staff discovered an irrepressible nostalgia for expansion baseball.

The Orioles were among the clubs the Jays had to beat to regain first place, and on August 23 the Jays kicked off a three-game set against them in good fettle, trouncing Baltimore 9-3. On the following night Jim Clancy carried a 3-1 lead into the bottom of the ninth but, with two out, got stuck, at which point Bobby Cox hooked him. It was a quite ordinary baseball situation – one of a team's regular starters does nearly an outing of sound late-summer work but cannot quite cap it, so the manager summons aid from his trusty bullpen to ice matters before they get out of hand. In this game, however, the pen iced nothing. Jay relievers twice surrendered the tying run and ultimately the winning run in the first loss of a disasterous slide that would eliminate them from the pennant race.

The widespread advent of the relief specialist in the 1950s has been among the more notable changes in baseball during its more than a century of history. Some changes have been of rules (e.g., the closed substitution rule of 1891, still in effect today; the diminution of the mound and strike zone in 1969), some have involved equipment (e.g., the lively ball introduced in 1921, the modern fielder's megamitt), and some have been of styles of play (e.g., the devolution, in the 1930s, and subsequent renaissance, in the 1960s, of the stolen base as an offensive weapon). The emergence of the professional fireman is in the latter category.

Relief pitching was not an unknown art prior to the 1950s. Mordechai Centennial Three-Finger Brown, for example, who hurled for the winningest club in modern major league history, the Chicago Cubs of the late 1900s, and who, in fact, had four fingers (and who was born in 1876, hence the eponym Centennial), was, like virtually all pitchers of his era, a starter but appeared from time to time in relief, logging in that capacity thirty wins and forty-eight saves. Such bullpen labour was not, however, regarded in Brown's epoch as a self-sufficient skill but dogsbody work which pitchers were occasionally required to do on behalf of rocked or injured colleagues, not a career a man aspired to. It was not until the late 1920s that the first great relief specialist appeared, a Texan named Firpo Marberry who pitched for the Washington Senators (on a staff which also included perhaps the greatest of all pitchers, Walter Johnson) and compiled fifty-three relief wins and 101 saves during a fourteen-year career. In Marberry's wake, in the 1930s and 1940s, a smattering of relievers plied their trade. The New York Yankees, the most formidable club in those decades, regularly stocked a stopper in the pen, first Fordham Johnny Murphy and later Joe Page, who combined from 1934 until 1950 for 180 Yankee saves and 114 relief wins. But relievers remained oddities, exceptions to the rule that a good pitcher's job was as a starter.

Then in 1952 a New York Giant rookie logged fifteen relief wins and eleven saves, beginning a career that would span twenty-one years with nine different clubs, during which he would establish himself as the prototype of the modern fireman and perhaps the finest reliever ever. By the time he retired in 1972 Hoyt Wilhelm had appeared in 1,070 games, more than any other pitcher in baseball history, and had recorded 227 saves, 123 relief wins, and a career earned run average of 2.52. And during Wilhelm's early heyday, the 1950s, it became axiomatic that a winning ballclub required an ace in the pen. In the 1960s professional relievers multiplied, and by the 1970s relief pitchers had become, like sluggers and twenty-game winners, stars in their own right, one of whose names was identified with every championship team: Fingers of the A's, Eastwick of the Reds, Lyle of the Yankees.

That no relief pitcher has yet been inducted to the Hall of Fame is in part because of their recency – only a handful have been eligible. Suspicion does linger, though, that Hoyt Wilhelm has been denied the required votes (he fell a scant fifteen ballots shy in 1984) in part because relief pitching remains, in the eyes of some of the electors, not quite a respectable trade, a kind of new-fangled specialism whose practitioners are not quite on a par with masters of the game's other skills. But if Wilhelm remains unbidden to the Hall – he may still make it* – it will be difficult to refuse admission, when his time comes, to Rollie Fingers, whose 301 saves to date (through 1983) may be a mark unmatched for a long, long time. (Fingers was not, however, the first fireman to be named a league's Most Valuable Player. Fingers, named MVP in the A.L. in 1982, was antedated by more than three decades by a National Leaguer, Wilhelm's precursor, Jim Konstanty, who won sixteen games in relief and saved twenty-two for the 1950 Whiz Kid Phillies.)

The Jays lost that August 24th game in Baltimore in the bottom of the tenth – we will return again later to the tale of this game, a baseball saga of bizarre proportion** – and on the following night they lost again in the tenth. The night after that they lost again in the tenth, and two days later they lost with two out in the ninth. The following day they lost again in the ninth, and the day after that they lost in the twelfth. The Bullpen Chainsaw Massacre. By the time it was over the Jays were in fifth place, six and a half games back, ground they would never recover. A small coterie of individuals masquerading as baseball fans, who would have been more at home during the Salem witch trials, sought to collar the bullpen's collapse on only one of its denizens, Joey McLaughlin. McLaughlin did fall upon hard times that week, but he was not alone. It was the full relief squad

* He did. (See Epilogue.)
** See Chapter Five.

that crumbled.

The Jays ended the season in fourth place, nine games out, in seventh place among all twenty-six major league clubs. Measured against mid-season's wild hopes that the club might win a flag, the outcome was uneventful. But measured against spring's expectations and against other expansion franchises in their seventh seasons, the Jays had distinguished themselves. Only one expansion team had managed a better seventh season and by only a two-game margin:

Expansion Club Records, Seventh Season

	W	L	PCT.	GB
Kansas City Royals (1975)	91	71	.562	—
Toronto Blue Jays (1983)	89	73	.550	2
Los Angeles/California Angels (1967)	84	77	.522	6½
Washington Senators/ Texas Rangers (1967)	76	85	.472	14½
Montreal Expos (1975)	75	87	.463	16
New York Mets (1968)	73	89	.451	18
Houston Colt 45s/Astros (1968)	72	90	.444	19
San Diego Padres (1975)	71	91	.438	20
Seattle Pilots/Milwaukee Brewers (1975)	68	94	.420	23
Seattle Mariners (1983)	60	102	.370	31

It had been a remarkable season, and for the Jays and their fans there could and would never be another year like it, the first winning season, a summer of surprises and delights and ridiculous hopes, the year the Jays earned respect. It was a season which changed everything, for now, on the eve of their eighth season, the Jays are a team expected to win. That, for both players and fans, is a whole new ball game.

TWO

Rumours and Blue Jays: On the Grapefruit Trail

We're just waiting on the pitchers to get ready. Like we do
every spring.
— Bobby Cox

March 13

Spring training has less to do with winning or losing than with players rehearsing their skills and with clubs shaping their rosters for opening day. A pitcher, for instance, may record a poor outing because he has used the occasion to woodshed a new changeup. Managers want a good look at how kids from the farm may fit in, and some don't. About twenty or twenty-one Jays are already tickmarked for the roster, so the main business in Florida this year, besides practice, is filling the other four or five slots.

One feature of spring training is rumours, often as not only batting-cage gossip, but interesting; they underline the main questions about a club. Among items from the Jay camp grapevine:

Rumour 1: Toronto will sign free agent Oscar Gamble as a portside d.h. and reserve outfielder. Since the December trade of Barry Bonnell to Seattle for southpaw Bryan Clark the Jays have had only four seasoned outfielders – Moseby, Barfield, Bell, and Collins – and want another outfielder on the roster. And Willie Aikens, acquired from Kansas City in January for Jorge Orta, is unable to begin work as Jays' lefty d.h. until his suspension by the Commissioner's office has ended, perhaps mid-May, perhaps not until next season. Hence there are two holes to fill, and Gamble might fill both although, while he is a good clutch hitter, he is only a passable outfielder, not ideal for the backup job. Best bet: the Jays will pass on Gamble and go with a kid from the farm, likely Mitch Webster, a switch-hitter with a tad of power and speed and a good glove.

Rumour 2: Righty pitcher Mike Morgan will be dealt to Cleveland so the Jays can keep kid infielder Kelly Gruber and assign him to the minors. The Jays picked up Gruber in the December minor league draft and, under the draft's rules, must carry him on their major league roster this sea-son or return him to the Indians. The Jays have had their eye on Gruber since 1980 when they nearly chose him in the first round of the amateur draft – they didn't, and Cleveland did – and would like to keep him, but as a minorleaguer. A contending club cannot afford a spot on the roster for the sake of hanging on to a kid as the Jays did in 1978 when they made room for Willie Upshaw, taken from the Yankees in that year's minor league draft. Upshaw hit only .237 and a single homer that season – he spent the next two years in the minors learning his trade – but the Jays' decision to keep him around that summer appears to have been a good one. And Morgan may be excess baggage. With Stieb, Clancy, Leal, Gott, and Doyle Alexander in camp, the Jays do not lack right-handed starters, and Dennis Lamp, Jackson, McLaughlin, and Jim Acker seem ahead of Morgan in line for righty bullpen jobs.

Rumour 3: General manager Pat Gillick, the Jays' principal author, is still hunting for a left-handed starter, and Pittsburgh has offered any one of three serviceable lefties – Larry McWilliams, John Candelaria, or John Tudor – for Jesse Barfield. Forget this one. However badly Gillick may want a southpaw, Barfield, among the best rightfielders in the league and the Jays' most explosive slugger, is not on the trading block. During the past two seasons Barfield has whacked forty-five homers in 782 at-bats, a round-tripper percentage of about 5.75. This pace, sustained through a career, would place Barfield beside such notables as R.M. Jackson and Duke Snider in baseball's record book. In any event, Gillick is unlikely to short the Jays by another outfielder.

Rumour 4: Toronto will swap Damaso Garcia, Jim Acker, and Geno Petralli to Texas for pitcher Danny Darwin and outfielder/third-sacker Larry Parrish. And the sun will rise in the west tomorrow. Granted, Texas needs a catcher, and Petralli is both a catcher and an organizational problem for the Jays: they have run out of options on him and cannot send him to the minors again. One problem here is that the Jays might be giving away more than they would be getting; Acker may turn out to be too good a pitcher to have been simply a bit of leavening in a deal.

Acker won his major league spurs in a game late last season against K.C. It was plain to opposing pitchers by then that Willie Upshaw was trouble, and Upshaw began to see a lot of hard tight ones. In the midst of this evening's festivities, one of the hard tight ones nailed Upshaw in the back as he tried to pull away. Acker trod to the mound for the next half-inning and cast a baleful eye at K.C. hitter Hal McRae, maybe the most hard-nosed player in the league. A moment later McRae was sprawled in the dirt beside the plate, and a moment after that McRae was en route to the mound to express firm views to young Acker about the offending projectile. Jay catcher Ernie Whitt had equally firm views about whether McRae's mission to the hillock should be summarily terminated and had barely begun to advise McRae of these when several dozen other ballplayers from each bench and various points on the field felt impelled to deliver their opinions too. Pandemonium ensued. The umpires presently sorted out the melange of Jay and Royal uniforms, restoring order. The message rookie Acker had delivered, of course, was that a pitcher who plunked Willie Upshaw was declaring open season on his own clubmates.

Another problem with this trade is that Gillick has talked mainly about acquiring pitchers and hitters who are lefties, and Darwin and Parrish are righties. But more to the point, Damaso Garcia is going nowhere for the moment; the Jays now have word on the condition of their young phenom shortstop Tony Fernandez, and the word is not good.

Shortstops are the glue who hold baseball defences together. It does not matter if a Rabbit Maranville or Marty Marion or Mark Belanger does not know one end of a bat from another; they would still have a place on any major league roster. The Cards' Ozzie Smith hit only .248 in 1982, the year St. Louis won the Series, but was seriously discussed as an MVP candidate. Smith's manager, Whitey Herzog, reckoned Smith's glove saved the Cards at least a run a game which, said Herzog, is as good as one scored.

The Jays limped through their first two summers with Hector Torres and Luis Gomez at shortstop. The fairest description of Torres is that he was a shortstop of limited range. Gomez was a little better but not enough to carry a .212 lifetime batting average, low even by shortstop standards. In December 1978 the Jays sent reliever Victor Cruz to Cleveland for Alfredo Griffin and a minor leaguer, a controversial trade. Cruz had been almost brilliant coming out of Toronto's pen that summer, his numbers Gossage-like: seven wins, three losses, nine saves, a 1.71 e.r.a., and fifty-one strikeouts in forty-seven innings pitched. Fresh from the minors, Griffin looked promising on paper, but kid shortstops are a chancy commodity.

In 1979 Cruz slumped to more human proportions; he has since been traded to Pittsburgh, then Texas, and has not had another season quite like his stunning rookie summer in T.O. Meanwhile Griffin shared American League rookie-of-the-year honours with Twin John Castino, batting .287, knocking 179 hits, stealing twenty bases, and making defensive plays Torres and Gomez would not even have thought about. During the next four seasons he played in more games than any Jay ever, 733, including streaks of 327 games started at shortstop and 347 consecutive games played. By the end of 1983 he was baseball's iron man, riding a longer string of consecutive games than any other major leaguer, a streak of note because middle infielders are especially vulnerable to injury. Not for nothing did Pat Gillick observe toward the close of that season that the Griffin-Cruz trade may have been the Jays' best in their seven-year history.

By 1983 Griffin was not yet a great shortstop, but he was

an awfully good one. Any doubts about his skills vanished with that July 18 game against the Royals. His range had always been exceptional; he is only five-eleven, but when he stretches for balls which appear to be past him and that would be past many shortstops, he often seems a lot taller. With experience he had curbed an adventurous tendency to rush his pegs, a habit that in earlier seasons had resulted in a lot of throwing errors; he seems to hate to swallow the ball.

At the plate he has been inconsistent, batting only .209 in 1981, the year of the Jays' Abominable Slump, and about .250 lifetime. He has still not curbed a habit for smacking soft popups; if he hit the ball down more, for line drives and a measure of infield hits, he might be a .300 hitter. Because of his quickness he has often been among the league leaders in triples, but he has been unable to turn his speed into the stolen bases the Jays hoped for; he has never quite mastered the crossover step. But he is a switch-hitter with some bat control: if not a Luke Appling, not a dead offensive liability either.

There is another dimension, too, to ballplayers besides offence and defence, less tangible – there are no stats in the matter – but no less important: their role in the process by which twenty-five men make a team and in a team's personality. Here Griffin seems near the heart of the Jays, respected by teammates and his manager and regarded with more affection than perhaps any other Jay by the fans.

In that Monday Night game against K.C., Griffin was all over the infield, snatching tough grounders deep in the hole and behind second base, snaring a couple of line drives that would have chewed up most infielders, rifling a bullet to first to gun down the fastest man in baseball, Willie Wilson. Yet he might not have been in the game at all – not, at least, according to Jay management's amended Plan. It was not that the Plan had gone wrong but that, so far as shortstop and the 1983 season were concerned, it had succeeded too well. Griffin played that night because at spring training four months earlier he had fought for his job, snatched it back from an heir apparent, a twenty-one-year-old kid from his own hometown, San Pedro de Macoris, Dominican Republic.*

In 1982 Tony Fernandez was the hottest property on any minor league infield. The Jays had signed him at sixteen and sent him to the farm. Over the years, his gifts became apparent – he fields effortlessly, hits line drives with alarming consistency, and runs the bases with quickness and grace – and Toronto's front office revised its plan: Griffin, who had seemed a fixture at shortstop for several years to come, was to be eased out of his job during 1983 and Fernandez assigned in his place. During the previous winter Jay management had even toyed with trading Griffin away to shore up the club's pitching but instead opted not to put all their shortstop eggs in the basket of a player who, however promising, had yet to be tested as a major-leaguer. Then, in Florida, Griffin worked so hard to keep his job that Fernandez ended up back in the minors in Syracuse, the Jays' triple-A club, on a kind of holding pattern. The Jays still might have traded Griffin early in the season but found themselves unexpectedly in first place and scrapping for a pennant, no time to break in a kid infielder.

So Alfredo Griffin remained the Jays' shortstop. And if during those first years the club had wanted dearly for a shortstop, their dilemma now was of another kind, an embarrassment of riches – a more upbeat problem but nearly as perplexing. There seemed little doubt, though, about who the shortstop of the future was, and as he played the

---

* Besides Griffin and Fernandez, two other major league shortstops, Rafael Ramirez of the Braves and Julio Franco of the Indians, are also natives of this small (pop. 15,000) Dominican town. And outfielder Pedro Guerrero of the Dodgers, pitcher Joaquin Andujar of the Cards, infielder Juan Samuel of the Phils, and outfielder George Bell of the Blue Jays also hail from San Pedro de Macoris, quite a bunch of ballplayers.

finest game of his career that July night, Alfredo Griffin, at the age of twenty-six, seemed about to lose his job to a hotshot kid.

Griffin's streak of games started at shortstop ended in September in Toronto. Fernandez came up from Syracuse at the close of the minor league season and, with the Jays now out of the pennant race, Bobby Cox gave the kid his first major league start. He did not disappoint, smacking a line-drive double, scoring two runs, and making a couple of nice fielding plays on which he showed off his signature as a shortstop, a quick flip-like throw. Cox replaced him with Griffin late in the game to keep Griffin's consecutive-game streak alive, but the handwriting on the wall was even clearer now. And it was unlikely a club with such visible holes in its pitching staff could afford the luxury of a first-string infielder warming the bench. Someone would be leaving, and it would not be Fernandez.

But it might not be Griffin either. Griffin can also play second base, had, in fact, played the position in tandem with Fernandez at short in the 1983 Caribbean all-star game. So the casualty might be Damaso Garcia, Revised Plan No. 2. This was not a notion universally accepted by Jay fans. As popular as Griffin was, he was not, like Garcia (yet another Dominican), a skilled second baseman by trade, and whatever his offensive possibilities, Griffin's numbers were no match for Garcia's. Garcia's only glaring weakness as a ballplayer is a penchant for free-swinging; he is likely to hack at anything he can put his bat on, reducing his utility as a leadoff man. To the extent shortstops and second basemen can be compared, on the other hand, Griffin was probably the better fielder, and Garcia, still piqued by a preseason salary quarrel with management, intimated he would not regret a trade away from Toronto. (He has since signed a five-year contract and made peace with the front office, now a happy Jay.) It was not a problem with an easy answer, and in the end the solution would likely depend on who had the highest market value in terms of filling Jay needs. While Garcia seemed, at first glance, the more valuable commodity, a club that required a shortstop might make an offer for Griffin which could not be refused. Thus matters stood at the close of the 1983 season.

It was about a month later that the Jays announced Tony Fernandez was hurt. Diving away from a collision with another Syracuse infielder in July, Fernandez had landed on his left hand and fractured a bone at the base of his thumb. Through the remainder of the minor league season and through his September stint with the Jays, Fernandez knew the hand was bothering him. But it was not until he went in October to a physician with his winter ball club in the D.R. for a shot of pain-killing cortisone that the injury finally was diagnosed. Happily, the fracture, already knitting, was mending cleanly. Fernandez's hand was put in a cast, and he and the Jays were advised to wait through winter for more definite news about when he would be able to play again.

The cast came off in February, and during the first couple of weeks of spring training Fernandez has fielded some soft grounders and hung around, waiting for more X-rays. These have now been taken; Fernandez is still not fit to play and will not be for at least a month, perhaps six weeks or longer. So Fernandez will start the season on the disabled list and, when he is able to play, will return to Syracuse on rehabilitation assignment.

One reason the Jays did as well as they did in 1983 was absence of serious injuries. Now, before the 1984 season has even begun, a key player is already on the d.l., and it is uncertain when he will be off. Meanwhile, there is no chance that Damaso Garcia will go to Texas or anywhere else, no matter how good an offer the Jays are tendered for him – not, at least, until Fernandez is in major league playing shape.

Alfredo Griffin, the Iron Man, will be at shortstop for the Jays for the start of another season.

March 15

Pat Gillick has confirmed that Garcia is going nowhere, but Gillick says he is still looking for more pitching, preferably a southpaw, and a left-hitting outfielder with power. Whether or where he will find such commodities is moot, and apart from free agent Gamble, whom *Sporting News* reports Gillick will probably sign but whom Gillick says he will not sign, he will have to trade in order to get them. The tricky part of trading is you have to give something up, and apart from a middling pitcher, Morgan, the Jays do not have a lot of surplus; a minor-leaguer like Petralli alone is unlikely to yield the kind of ballplayer Gillick wants.

There was apparently a trade feeler received from Detroit, who would like Jim Gott and are trying to unload a modestly talented right-hitting outfielder. Why they should think Toronto would be interested in such a swap is a matter for conjecture. Clubs are particularly careful about trading within their own division, especially with a team they may have to beat come September. The Tigers are the other comers in the A.L. East this season, and they and the Jays are unlikely to do each other any favours.

Philadelphia is said to have expressed interest in Cliff Johnson, although Johnson may have undone this a couple of days ago with an infelicitous outing at first base. Because the N.L. has no d.h., clubs in that circuit prefer bench-muscle who can field a position with at least minimal competence. Johnson has caught and played some first and outfield during his career, but it has been his lumber, never his glove, for which he has received his paycheques, particularly as he has aged. His work at first this week disabused the Phils of any notion he could, if need arose, sub in that slot.

It is not, in any event, clear that the Jays have any interest in trading Johnson. As the club's righty d.h. he drove in seventy-six runs last year. (The left side of the combo, Orta, drove in thirty-eight, yielding the best net total in the league.) And he is a strong clubhouse influence – at thirty-six, the Jays' senior citizen and one of three Jays who have been to the World Series. (The others are Alexander and Aikens; and Lamp and Martinez have been as far as the league pennant series.) Older ballplayers with this kind of experience are a steadying influence on a young club like Toronto, striving for contention. The Phils do, however, have one of the exact commodities on Pat Gillick's shopping list, a southpaw reliever with good credentials, Willie Hernandez, who may be available because the Phils have another strong lefty in their pen, Al Holland. Johnson for Hernandez? Mm, tricky.*

That, for the moment, about covers the rumours.

The Jays' past trading record has not been bad. There has been the occasional clunker – the swap of Alan Ashby to Houston for Mark Lemongello and a couple of minor-leaguers comes to mind. The less said about Lemongello's brief stay in Toronto – won one, lost nine, a 6.29 e.r.a. in eighty-three innings pitched – the better. His main skill appears to have been demolishing furniture. Ashby, meanwhile, has done five seasons' journeyman service behind the plate for the Astros. But more often the Jays' trades have worked out.

Eight of the current flock, besides Griffin, Clark, and Aikens, were acquired in swaps. Garcia and McLaughlin arrived in 1979 in a two-chapter deal that also yielded Barry Bonnell: Rick Cerone, Tommy Underwood (now an Oriole), and a minor-leaguer were traded to the Yankees in November for Garcia, Chris Chambliss, and Paul Mirabella – the key player in the swap was Cerone; New York

---

* The Jays did not deal for Hernandez, and the Detroit Tigers did, a trade that was among the critical factors in the year's A.L. race. (See Chapter Twelve.) The Tigers acquired in the same three-cornered swap with the Phils and Giants first baseman Dave Bergman, who also proved to be a handy addition to their roster.

urgently required a catcher following the untimely death of Thurmon Munson. Then in December, Chambliss and Luis Gomez were dealt to Atlanta for McLaughlin, Bonnell, and a minor-leaguer. Another trade with New York in December 1982 yielded Collins, Morgan, and a minor-leaguer in return for reliever Dale Murray and a minor-leaguer. And Jackson, Martinez, Mulliniks, and Johnson were acquired in one-for-one trades: Jackson from the Mets for Bob Bailor in 1980; Martinez from Milwaukee for a minor-leaguer in 1981; Mulliniks from the Royals for pitcher Phil Huffman in 1982; and Johnson from the A's for Al Woods in 1982.

The Mulliniks-Huffman trade raises an essential item of Blue Jay *arcana* in which the principal figure is one Ricardo Adolpho Jacabo Carty, yet another native of San Pedro de Macoris, D.R., and the principal in a trading sequence which resembles a Biblical genealogy – Noah begat Japeth who begat Magog and so forth. Toronto took Rico Carty in the expansion draft from the unprotected roster of the Cleveland Indians, who had apparently not anticipated the Jays to opt for an aging and halt-legged erstwhile slugger and who, chagrined, wanted Carty back. Toronto returned him, for the price of Rick Cerone and outfielder John Lowenstein. A couple of months later – the Jays had still yet to play a ball game – Cleveland decided they wanted Lowenstein back, too, so the Jays exchanged him for Hector Torres – in retrospect, another clunker. The following year the Jays reacquired Carty in a trade for minor league pitcher Dennis Debarr, and Carty had his best season since 1970. Late in the summer Toronto swapped him to Oakland for Huffman and Willie Horton, then that winter acquired Carty, now a free agent, again, his third transmogrification as a Jay. By then his gifts had begun to fail him, and that year, 1979, was his last in major league baseball, one of the most skilled natural hitters of his era. His main service to Toronto, however, was not with a bat but as a trading commodity whose residue on the current roster, through subsequent trades, includes in whole or in part Garcia, McLaughlin, Mulliniks, and Clark.

The remaining Jays have come to the club through the 1976 expansion draft, minor league drafts, the Jays' own scouting and farm system, and free agency:

• The expansion draft survivors are Iorg, Clancy, and Whitt, taken, respectively, from the organizations of New York, Texas, and Boston. Whitt and Iorg did not come up from the farm until 1980, and so Clancy is the sole remaining Jay from the club's first season.

• Three veteran Jays besides Upshaw were acquired in the minor league draft: Bell, taken from the Phils in 1980 (the Phils did not protect Bell on their roster but tried to hide him on a Dominican winter-league B-team and were so incensed at his loss they fired their farm director); Gott, taken from the Cards in 1981; and Acker, taken from Atlanta in 1982.

• Stieb, Moseby, Barfield, Leal, Fernandez, and five minor-leaguers who may catch on with the Jays when they come north later this month or sometime during the season – Webster, Petralli, Stan Clarke, Ron Shepherd, and Fred Manrique – are products of the Jays' scouting and farm organization. Clarke is a southpaw reliever, who has been throwing well in exhibition outings. Shepherd is a right-hitting outfielder with some power and a trace of speed. Manrique is a middle-infielder.

• Finally, two Jays have been signed as free agents: Alexander, after he was cut by the Yankees last June, and Lamp.

March 16

The signing of Lamp was the Jays' biggest move this winter and the club's first serious plunge into the free-agent market for a player deemed essential to the roster's bedrock. The Master Plan had provided offence, starting pitching, and defence, but had left the gap in the bullpen, and it was to help plug that gap that Lamp was signed.

Lamp began his career as a starter with the Chicago Cubs, with whom he posted modest numbers: a .406 winning percentage and an e.r.a. of slightly more than 4.00 over four seasons; it was as a Cub, in 1979, that he surrendered Lou Brock's 3,000th hit. He was then traded across town to the White Sox, where he was used increasingly in relief and with whom his numbers improved: .543 and 3.45 over three years, including a very good year, 1981, in which his e.r.a. was third best in the league. By the second half of 1983 he was specializing in short relief, and he saved fifteen games that season for the division-winning Sox. He is a control pitcher whose out pitch is a sinker that yields ground balls, a plus insofar as the Jays play tight infield, a minus insofar as Exhibition Stadium has artificial turf on which grounders that might be playable on the grass in Chicago's parks sometimes slip through for hits.

Lamp is not the legendary Goose, who had been the Jays' first choice for the stopper job, nor is he in the class of relievers like K.C.'s Dan Quisenberry or the Cards' Bruce Sutter. He is more a journeyman ballplayer. But with Jackson and McLaughlin he may be able to help do the job, and his acquisition gives the Jay relief corps more depth (on paper, at least) than it has had in any past season. Arguably, Lamp may be a better long-term investment than Gossage, a power pitcher whose gifts may quickly fail him as he ages; time will tell.

The Jays' other principal off-season acquisitions were Bryan Clark and Willie Aikens. Like Lamp, Clark was acquired to strengthen the bullpen. He throws hard stuff, mainly fastballs and sliders, and has a history of control problems. Seattle used him last season primarily in middle relief and as a starter; he won seven, lost ten, and had an e.r.a., within the realm of respectability in the Mariners' Kingdome, of 3.94. He didn't come cheaply. Bonnell batted .304 for the Jays over the last two seasons and is a good outfielder with a strong arm. But the Jays wanted to make more room in the outfield for Bell, and Bonnell is too young and too good a ballplayer for a bench job; with Seattle he will be a regular.

The acquisition of Aikens was problematic. The ex-K.C. slugger is currently serving a three-month sentence for a misdemeanor narcotics offense in a Texas minimum security "correctional facility." The Jays arranged the Aikens-Orta deal in December, after Aikens' conviction, but before his one-year suspension by the Commissioner's office. If the suspension is lifted when it is reviewed in May, the Jays will have lost Aikens for only about three dozen games. There is no question he will be missed for those games. The A.L. East may well be won this year by the club that gets most quickly in front of the pack, and the absence of a lefty d.h. who hit .302, knocked twenty-three homers, and drove in seventy-two runs in some 400 at-bats last year is no small matter. What will hurt much more, however, will be loss of Aikens for the season if the suspension is not lifted. This will not spell the end of Aikens' career; he is only thirty, and a lot of ballplayers have come back from a year's absence to play good ball again – some who lost time because of injury, others because of war; one of baseball's large questions marks is the career record Ted Williams might have compiled had he not lost nearly five seasons in the midst of his career to service as a Marine pilot. But the Jays' chances of winning the division are significantly diminished without Aikens. Hence, the flirtation with Gamble.

March 26

The Detroit Tigers have acquired Willie Hernandez from the Phils, and so the Tigers' bullpen, until now reckoned iffy, all at once seems strong and deep. Hernandez and the Tigers' other main relievers, Aurelio Lopez and Doug Bair, both righties, combined for twenty-six wins, sixteen losses, thirty-one saves, and a 3.19 e.r.a. last season. The trade does not upset many predictions about how the A.L. East will turn out this year. Detroit, commonly picked to finish second, has been at least slightly overrated and may still have an uphill fight to catch last year's champs, the Orioles. But Hernandez does give the Tigers a fresh edge in a race in which a couple of games one way or the other may be the difference among four or five clubs.

Forecasts for the Jays range from first, in *Sport* magazine, to fifth, in *Sporting News*; if fifteen or so different forecasts are averaged, they place third. The Brewers and Yanks are next, in no particular order, and the Red Sox and Indians place sixth and seventh. The dark horse may be Boston, who will win a few ball games and may upset an apple cart or two.*

Forecasting baseball is tricky. There are ways in which no team sport is more predictable. American League batters will hit about .262 and knock about 2,000 home runs this season. The pitchers will give up about four earned runs a game and throw about 585 wild pitches. Teams will, by October, lodge in their inevitable niches, their fortunes now already largely determined before play is even underway. The length of the season and logic and inexorability of its processes ensure that accidents do not happen and yield simple certitudes: skill and sound play will be rewarded; mistakes will be taxed justly and inflexibly. The precision of the game's statistics reflects one of its basic truths: luck is irrelevant – or, more accurately, in Branch Rickey's words, "Luck is the residue of design."

Yet no team sport has more unpredictable wild cards. Injuries and astonishing rookies may upset all calculations, and no matter how much of the game one has seen, it has a

---

* With respect to at least second place, the A.L. East did turn out to be tight; the division's four runners-up were bunched, at season's end, within four games of one another. And the Red Sox did have a stronger summer than many forecasters predicted. As for the notion, however, that the Tigers may have been a little overrated – mm, well, it did seem that way at the time.

constant capacity to startle. Odds are good the surprises will occur at moments one least expects them. The more one sees of the game, the less one is sure of, and the more one appreciates how hard it is and how much it is played not with the body but the head. It seems at once both that a single careless pitch or missed cutoff can shape the outcome of an entire season but also that no one event has meaning outside the web of a season as a piece. Hence, another of the game's basic truths, this time in Yogi Berra's words: "In baseball, you don't know nothin'."

April 4

Amid a final flurry of roster-shuffles and rumours the Jays have pared their club to the twenty-five players who will take the field against Seattle tonight.

Items:

• Oscar Gamble will likely return to the Yankees. The Jays, in any event, do not seem to need him. An arbitrator's decision about two players suspended by the Commissioner's office for reasons identical to Willie Aikens means Aikens will be in yoke by mid-May.

• Stan Clarke, after his hot start, cooled off considerably. Word is he has the skills but puts too much pressure on himself.

• Joey McLaughlin posted the best spring numbers of any Jay pitcher, but neither Cox nor Gillick is said to be happy about his work, in spite of his numbers.

• George Bell batted about .550, with a lot of r.b.i.'s and extra-base hits, during the first few weeks of the exhibition schedule, and Cox has inked him into the starting lineup for tonight's game in Seattle.

• Petralli stuck with the club as an occasional hitter and reserve fielder. Mitch Webster will be the fifth outfielder. And Kelly Gruber will stay in spite of an indistinguished spring showing: a .122 b.a. and nine errors in the field. Gillick does not want to return Gruber to Cleveland and characterized the Indians' notions about possible deals for him "ridiculous" (they asked for Gott). When Fernandez and Aikens are able to play, Petralli, Webster, and Gruber will get another hard look.

The toughest choices were on the pitching side. The brightest spot among Jay hurlers this spring has been a twenty-two-year-old southpaw, Jimmy Key, a Jay farm system product who pitched double-A and triple-A last year. Key came to camp as a non-roster player and won three games, and reasoning from the as-long-as-the-kid-is-hot principle, Gillick and Cox first indicated Key would make the cut. They then had sober second thoughts and announced he would be returned to Syracuse. On third thought they decided to keep him after all. The spot Key took had been Bryan Clark's and it will be Clark who goes to the minors. Gillick and Cox voiced confidence in Clark throughout spring training in spite of his uncertain performance: an e.r.a. of nearly 10.00 and nine walks, five wild pitches, and a hit batsman in sixteen innings' work. But in the end they decided to go with a pitcher who can at least put the ball over the plate, which Key does. Stan Clarke, too, will go to Syracuse, though he may be back later in the season. Finally, Mike Morgan is gone, outrighted to Syracuse and unlikely to return as a Jay.

THREE

Jays '84: Roster and Reserves

Opening Day Line-Up vs. Seattle Mariners, April 4, 1984

	BORN	MAJOR LEAGUE CLUBS
2B Damaso GARCIA	2/7/57, Moca, D.R.	New York Yankees (1978–79, 29 Games)
		Toronto Blue Jays (1980–83, 482 G.)
3B Rance MULLINIKS	1/15/56, Tulare, Cal.	California Angels (1977–79, 150 G.)
		Kansas City Royals (1980–81, 60 G.)
		Toronto Blue Jays (1982–83, 241 G.)
CF Lloyd MOSEBY	11/5/59, Portland, Ark.	Toronto Blue Jays (1980–83, 512 G.)
1B Willie UPSHAW	4/27/57, Blanco, Tex.	Toronto Blue Jays (1978, 1980–83, 610 G.)
DH Cliff JOHNSON	7/22/47, San Antonio, Tex.	Houston Astros (1972–77, 376 G.)
		New York Yankees (1977–79, 160 G.)
		Cleveland Indians (1979–80, 126 G.)
		Chicago Cubs (1980, 68 G.)
		Oakland A's (1981–82, 157 G.)
		Toronto Blue Jays (1983, 142 G.)
LF George BELL	10/21/59, San Pedro de Macoris, D.R.	Toronto Blue Jays (1981, 1983, 99 G.)
RF Jesse BARFIELD	10/29/59, Joliet, Ill.	Toronto Blue Jays (1981–83, 292 G.)
C Ernie WHITT	6/13/52, Detroit, Mich.	Boston Red Sox (1976, 8 G.)
		Toronto Blue Jays (1977–78, 1980–83, 433 G.)
SS Alfredo GRIFFIN	3/6/57, San Pedro de Macoris, D.R.	Cleveland Indians (1976–78, 31 G.)
		Toronto Blue Jays (1979–83, 733 G.)
RHP Jim CLANCY	12/18/55, Chicago, Ill.	Toronto Blue Jays (1977–83, 186 G.)

On the Bench

	BORN	MAJOR LEAGUE CLUBS
RHP Jim ACKER	9/24/58, Freer, Tex.	Toronto Blue Jays (1983, 38 G.)
RHP Doyle ALEXANDER	9/4/50, Cordova, Ala.	Los Angeles Dodgers (1971, 17 G.); Baltimore Orioles (1972–76, 137 G.); New York Yankees (1976, 1982–83, 43 G.); Texas Rangers (1977–79, 88 G.); Atlanta Braves (1980, 35 G.); San Francisco Giants (1981, 24 G.); Toronto Blue Jays (1983, 17 G.)
OF Dave COLLINS	10/20/52, Rapid City, S.D.	California Angels (1975–76, 192 G.); Seattle Mariners 1977, 120 G.); Cincinnati Reds (1978–81, 463 G.); New York Yankees (1982, 111 G.); Toronto Blue Jays (1983, 118 G.)
RHP Jim GOTT	8/3/59, Hollywood, Cal.	Toronto Blue Jays (1982–83, 64 G.)
IF Kelly GRUBER	2/26/62, Bellaire, Tex.	
IF Garth IORG	10/12/54, Arcata, Cal.	Toronto Blue Jays (1978, 1980–83, 420 G.)
LHP Jimmy KEY	4/22/61, Huntsville, Ala.	
RHP Roy Lee JACKSON	5/1/54, Opelika, Ala.	New York Mets (1977–80, 40 G.); Toronto Blue Jays (1981–83, 136 G.)
RHP Dennis LAMP	9/23/52, Los Angeles, Cal.	Chicago Cubs (1977–80, 127 G.); Chicago White Sox (1981–83, 120 G.)
RHP Louis LEAL	3/21/57, Barquisimeto, Ven.	Toronto Blue Jays (1980–83, 115 G.)
RHP Joey MCLAUGHLIN	7/11/56, Tulsa, Okla.	Atlanta Braves (1977, 1979, 40 G.)

C Buck MARTINEZ   11/7/48, Redding, Cal.   Toronto Blue Jays (1980-83, 189 G.)
Kansas City Royals (1969-71, 1973-77, 361 G.)
Milwaukee Brewers (1978-80, 234 G.)

C Geno PETRALLI   9/25/59, Sacramento, Cal.   Toronto Blue Jays (1981-83, 229 G.)

RHP Dave STIEB   7/22/57, Santa Ana, Cal.   Toronto Blue Jays (1982-83, 22 G.)

OF Mitch WEBSTER   5/16/59, Larned, Kan.   Toronto Blue Jays (1979-83, 151 G.)
Toronto Blue Jays (1983, 11 G.)

On Hold*

IF Willie AIKENS   10/14/54, Seneca, S.C.   California Angels (1977, 1979, 158 G.)
Kansas City Royals (1980-83, 511 G.)

LHP Bryan CLARK   7/12/56, Madera, Cal.   Seattle Mariners (1981-83, 107 G.)

IF Tony FERNANDEZ   8/6/62, San Pedro de Macoris, D.R.   Toronto Blue Jays (1983, 15 G.)

*Five other players also joined the Jays during the season:

C Toby HERNANDEZ   11/30/58, Calaboza, Ven.

OF Rick LEACH   5/4/57, Ann Arbor, Mich.   Detroit Tigers (1981-83, 235 G.)

IF Fred MANRIQUE   11/5/61, Bolivar, Ven.   Toronto Blue Jays (1981, 14 G.)

RHP Ron MUSSELMAN   11/11/54, Wilmington, N.C.   Seattle Mariners (1982, 12 G.)

OF Ron SHEPHERD   10/27/60, Longview, Tex.

FOUR

Barnstorming and China Cups

You can't sit on a lead and run a few plays into the line and just kill the clock. You've got to throw the ball over the goddamn plate and give the other man his chance.
— Earl Weaver

April 9

After five games the Jays are three and two. They might easily be five and oh, but leads carried into the late innings have twice been squandered. Both catastrophes occurred after Jay starters had acquitted themselves with distinction.

Worrisome? No and yes. No, because it is much too soon to make any judgements about the course of the season. The Orioles, for instance, have won none and lost four so far, a lousy index of how their summer will turn out; they are notoriously late starters. But, yes, because those two games are gone irrevocably, and if the Jay season comes down to the wire lost by a nose, those games and any others like them will haunt the winter that follows. (The Tigers, notably, have made no mistakes yet and have won five and lost none.) And, yes, because it means the Jay bullpen might yet be Adventureland, which may make the club edgy, and edgy baseball is nearly always losing baseball.

The Jays opened their season in the Seattle Mausoleum (a.k.a. the Kingdome) against their sibling club, the Mariners, who in their first seven seasons have made little progress and in 1983 lost more games, 102, than any other team in the majors. Seattle has gone nowhere because the club's front-office management has been constantly in flux and marked by unsound judgement (budgeting miserly initial resources for a scouting system, for example, and allowing some pretty good ballplayers to slip away rather than signing them to long-term contracts – among them pitchers Floyd Bannister, Rick Honeycutt, and Shane Rawley, infielder Julio Cruz, and outfielder Tom Paciorek). The Mariners have entered the current season with some good young arms, some power, and some eagerness to prove they are not fish in a barrel. They are unlikely to be a dominant force in the league, but they will not lose as docilely as last year.

No one was quite ready for the tense pip Game One turned out to be. After a lapse of six months since any serious baseball had occurred we were abruptly in the midst of a grinding pitchers' duel between Jim Clancy for the Jays and fastballer Mike Moore for Seattle. The only scoring in the first six innings was a solo shot parked in the bleachers by Ernie Whitt in the third, and a measure of Clancy's strength was that, of the eighteen outs he recorded over those frames, six were K's and seven were groundouts. The Mariners scattered a few singles but otherwise barely put the ball out of the infield, and by mid-game Clancy was cruising in the kind of easy groove that makes opposing hitters look like they are swinging at gumdrops.

The top of the seventh was highlighted by the play of Cliff Johnson, first at bat, then on the base paths. Johnson's main tradecraft is the longball, and the only thing more fun than watching him go downtown is watching when the count runs against him and he protects the plate and his at-bat by spraying foul balls this way and that. On this occasion the tactic yielded a walk. George Bell, behind him, rammed a double to left (Bell has shown few signs of flagging from his torrid Florida hitting pace) on which Johnson, no speed-demon, would ordinarily have stopped at third. On this night, however, he did not. Seattle left-fielder Gorman Thomas, plagued this spring by trouble with the rotator cuff in his throwing arm, had been in obvious pain on a peg from deep in the outfield earlier in the game, and Johnson, egged on by Jay third-base coach Jimy Williams, never stopped motoring as he lumbered around third. He then executed a perfect hook-slide – Ty Cobb could not have done it better – to score under the throw that finally did arrive. It was – first the walk, then the run – the season's first chestnut, to be stored for next winter when, again, the game will exist only in memory.*

---

* Shortly after this game Thomas went onto the disabled list and did not return to the active roster for the duration of the season. Seattle, who had been counting on his power, badly missed him. Whether he will ever play again is uncertain.

In the bottom of the seventh Clancy began to labour; as strong as he had looked through the first six innings, it was, after all, still April, when most pitchers are not yet strong enough to hold their rhythm for an entire game. He walked the lead-off batter, who was erased on a double play, then surrendered a homer which halved the Jay lead. In the eighth he gave up two more walks, and, with two out, Bobby Cox dispatched his first call to the pen for shiny new stopper Dennis Lamp. On his very first pitch Lamp suckered Barry Bonnell to top an easy grounder to third and end the threat. The Jays and their fans will be specially watchful of damage Bonnell does or does not do Toronto this season; players do enjoy inflicting discomfort on teams which have turned them from the fold. Last year's ex-Jay-turned-Jay-basher-of-the-year was Twin hurler Ken Schrom who threw a handful of innings with Toronto in 1980 and 1982. In 1983 Schrom beat Dave Stieb three times – *nobody* beats Dave Stieb three times – and recorded a 1.96 e.r.a. against his old club.*

Gorman Thomas giveth, and Gorman Thomas taketh away. The ailing leftfielder was Seattle's first hitter in the bottom of the ninth and whacked a double. Lamp got an out, then gave up a single which moved the runner to third and another single which scored him, the tying run. Seattle notched the winner in the bottom of the tenth on an exceeding ill-timed walk, a sacrifice bunt, and a sparkling single to right.

And so the evening's bottom line was one stroke in the loss column for Dennis Lamp and for the Jays, and Jim Clancy ended up with nothing to show for nearly eight innings' sound work but a tired arm. In fairness, the fault was not wholly Lamp's. Twice in the game's earlier frames George Bell was nailed for excessively exuberant baserunning, and on two other occasions Jays who reached

* Bonnell was, for the season, harmless against the Jays; his b.a. vs. Jay hurling was a diminutive .100.

41

third base with less than two out died there. Then in the top of the tenth Barfield led off with a single, Whitt was hit by a pitch to move the runner to second, and Griffin lofted a long fly to left to move the runner to third. Again, he died there. A club which gets two men on with none out in the tenth, does not score, and loses by a run cannot blame all its woes on the pen.

To wit, Game One – a pretty good ball game but, in the end, a heartbreaker. One hundred and sixty-one to go.

In Game Two the Jay bats thundered to life. Mariner pitcher Jim Beattie has done pretty well against Toronto in past, but he looked this evening as though he had come north from spring training too soon. The Jays rocked him and five other Seattle ballsmen for nineteen hits, including a massive homer by Lloyd Moseby and a more orthodox homer by Willie Upshaw, and thirteen runs. (Moseby's blast was a rope still rising as it smacked of the upper-deck facing in straightaway centre.) Luis Leal did allow four runs in five frames but in large part because his clubmates left him to go cold in the dugout during a couple of thirty-minute half-innings while they carried on their offensive pyrotechnics. The night's nicest piece of hitting was a modest clutch single by Alfredo Griffin with two out in the second, which drove in the match's first two runs before anyone knew it would turn out to be a laugher, exactly the kind of timely hitting that wins not only ball games but pennants.

On to California, barnstorming.

The California Angels are the creation of singing cowboy and multimillionaire businessman Gene Autry, who has made it his mission to cop a World Series flag for Anaheim before he gits along to the last roundup. Twice, in 1979 and 1982, he has come close, but the Orioles and Brewers, fastest bats in the East those years, had other ideas. Autry, a realist, has recognized he does not have a whole lot of time left to accomplish his purpose, and so his Plan has not emphasized patience. No owner except perhaps Yankee *Fuhrer* George Steinbrenner has been as active in the free agent market, and the California bunkhouse is stocked with hired guns. They are a wizening lot, the Angels, baseball elders who have been around, among them Tommy John, Ken Forsch, Reggie Jackson, Rod Carew, Bob Boone, Bobby Grich, which lends them two qualities. They bruise more easily and heal less quickly than whippersnappers – injuries decimated the Angels in 1983. But they are always dangerous; experience matters in baseball more than in any other sport, and given clubs of roughly equal skills, age will nearly always win in the end.

The Jays rolled into Anaheim with their bats still singing and by the third inning of Game Three had already scored six runs. This evening's nice piece of clutch hitting was by Upshaw, who knocked a one-out two-r.b.i. base-hit in the top of the first. They tallied two more in the fifth. Trouble was, though, starter Doyle Alexander did not have his good stuff; the Angels were scoring too. They had five by the fifth, at which juncture Bobby Cox had seen enough of Alexander and replaced him with Roy Jackson. With two out in the sixth Jackson walked the bases full; the bullpen was again playing Russian Roulette. The next hitter was Rod Carew, possessor of the major leagues' highest active lifetime batting average (.331). Carew hits left. Bobby Cox looked to his pen and observed but a single southpaw, young Jimmy Key. As long as the kid is hot....

Key's first major league pitch was a strike, his second a ball, and his third also a ball, a curve that kicked dirt in front of the plate. Ernie Whitt blocked it to prevent a run from scoring and adjourned to the mound for brief words with Master Key on the topic of throwing strikes. Master Key blinked and nodded. Master Key threw a strike. Carew topped it to short and the inning was over, three l.o.b.'s.

In the seventh inning Key faced Reggie Jackson, Doug

DeCinces, and Fred Lynn, a troublesome lot in the best of times, and retired them one-two-three. The Angels in the eighth: again, one-two-three. In the ninth: once more, one-two-three. Meanwhile, the Jays notched three more. (Cliff Johnson, who entered the game sick with a mild bout of flu, whacked a pair of two-run homers during the evening.) Final: Jays 11, Angels 5; Jimmy Key 0, 0, 0, 1 – no runs, no hits, no men on base, and a win, his first major league decision.

Game Four, Dave Stieb's first start, was a model of economy. When Stieb is on his game – when his fastball has its movement – he seems to have come down from a higher league, and for most of seven innings the Angels were meat. He did scatter a few inconsequential singles and a walk, but his only real mistake was a hanger which Doug DeCinces took downtown, a solo. Meanwhile, Upshaw and Moseby each tagged his season's second homer; and Dennis Lamp did his job, closing matters out with two innings of flawless relief.

Until the roof caved in, Game Five was nearly as tidy. It was an occasion of minor weight in the history of the Jay franchise; it marked the club's first chance since the early outings of Year One to go above .500 against another A.L. club. Toronto had ended 1983 only two games in arrears against California – thirty-nine wins, forty-one losses – and now was even; a win would have special meaning. Jim Gott was slated to start but was scratched at post-time – flu – for Jim Acker, who tore a leaf from Stieb's book and pitched seven good innings. The Angels bunched a few singles for a run in the fifth, but the Jays tallied one in the seventh and two in the eighth, again with a nice piece of clutch hitting, a two-r.b.i. double by Garcia. Roy Jackson replaced Acker in the eighth, got an out, gave up a single to Carew and got another out, and up stepped Reggie Jackson, who took a ball. Ernie Whitt called for the next pitch on Jackson's hands, his sucker zone, but Jackson (Roy) went down and slightly away, the kind of pitch Jackson (Reggie) in his

44

heyday gobbled like M & M's. *Thwock* and bye-bye. Tie game. Popping a coin into Jackson (Reggie)'s power slot was not, however, Jackson (Roy)'s most unforgivable mistake of the afternoon; this, rather, was the very *next* pitch, a fat one to DeCinces (Doug), who rammed it past the leftfield fence. The Jays will have to wait until they visit Texas later in the week to go above .500 against another A.L. club.

Jays' Record Against A.L. Clubs, 1977–1983

VS.	W	L	PCT.	GB
Texas Rangers	39	39	.500	—
California Angels	39	41	.487	1
Seattle Mariners	34	40	.459	3
Chicago White Sox	37	44	.457	3½
Oakland A's	36	45	.444	4½
Cleveland Indians	36	50	.419	7
Detroit Tigers	37	55	.402	9
Kansas City Royals	30	46	.395	8
New York Yankees	33	54	.379	10½
Milwaukee Brewers	34	58	.370	12
Minnesota Twins	26	48	.351	11
Boston Red Sox	29	57	.337	14
Baltimore Orioles	27	62	.303	17½

April 11
The venerable A's, currently of Oakland, have fielded in their eighty-three years some of baseball's most and least distinguished teams. Their history has been twined with the personalities of two men, Cornelius McGillicuddy and Charles O. Finley. Connie Mack, born in 1862 and manager of the Philadelphia Athletics from 1901 until 1950, created two of the game's most formidable clubs: the A's of 1910 to 1914 who won four pennants, three World Series, and numbered on their roster two Hall of Fame infielders, Eddie Collins and Frank "Home Run" Baker, and three Hall of Fame pitchers, Chief Bender, Herb Pennock, and

Eddie Plank; and the A's of 1929 to 1931 who won three pennants, two Series, and included five more Hall of Famers, sluggers Jimmie Foxx and Al Simmons, catcher Mickey Cochrane, and pitchers Lefty Grove and Waite Hoyt. (The 1931 A's are members of one of baseball's most select elites: the .700 clubs. Only eight teams in modern major league history have played seasons of .700 ball, and four did so prior to 1910 – the 1902 and 1909 Pittsburgh Pirates and 1906 and 1907 Chicago Cubs. The others, besides the A's, were the 1927 and 1939 New York Yankees and, most recently, the 1954 Cleveland Indians.)

Mack's A's also, however, had less successful campaigns; from 1935 until 1950, when Mack retired at age eighty-eight (shortly after his retirement, in 1955, the franchise moved to Kansas City), the A's were the A.L.'s doormats ten times and escaped from the second division only once, in 1948. Mack himself was a legend, a shrewd businessman and a repository of baseball lore (he had begun his playing career in 1886 as a catcher for the Washington Senators, then of the National League), a lean, angular man who managed his clubs from a shady corner of the dugout clad in a dark business suit, starched collar, and straw boater and manoeuvred his fielders with wags of a furled scorecard. There has never, ever, been a figure in baseball quite like the Grand Old Man of Shibe Park.

Finley was another story entirely, a manic self-made millionaire who purchased the franchise in the late 1960s, moved it to Oakland, and put together one of the fine recent clubs, the A's of 1972 to 1974. A common measure of excellence in any sport is defence of a championship not only once but twice; Finley's A's won three consecutive World Series, an accomplishment unmatched by any other ballclub except the New York Yankees who won four straight from 1936 to 1939 and five straight from 1949 to 1953.

Finley's A's were quite nearly an all-star team unto themselves – Catfish Hunter, Vida Blue, Blue Moon Odom, and Ken Holtzman on the mound, Rollie Fingers and Darold Knowles in the pen, Gene Tenace, Bert Campaneris, and Sal Bando in the infield, Joe Rudi, Reggie Jackson, and Bill North in the outfield – and common wisdom was that the bond that knotted together this fractious clan of proud and unkindred spirits as a team was hatred of their stormy architect. In the end he broke them up, auctioned them off to the highest bidder – liquidated his assets – rather than submit to the new rules of salary bargaining which, in the wake of abolition of the reserve clause, meant ballplayers were no longer chattel. By 1977 the A's had slumped to their division's bottom, winning fewer games that year than any other A.L. club but one, the first-season Toronto Blue Jays.

Now under new ownership, with a roster stocked with a mix of youngsters, spare-part trade and free agent acquisitions, and a handful of talented remainders from the waning days of the Finley era, the A's are again reviving.

The Jays split two with Oakland, 4-3 (A's) and 3-0 (Jays). Baseball seasons are like jigsaw puzzles. At-bats, innings, games are pieces. The scant pieces of this year's Jay puzzle so far available have some consistency. The offence is there; the Jays have rattled out seventy-three hits, thirty-eight runs, and ten homers in seven games. The starters are mostly doing their jobs. Clancy and Leal have pitched twice and have e.r.a.'s of 1.84 and 3.08, Stieb and Acker were barely hittable in their single outings, and only Alexander has had trouble, not so worrisome because he is the staff's grizzled vet, unlikely to be rattled by occasional hard times; last year he had thirteen decisions for the Jays – six straight losses followed by seven consecutive wins. And the defence, the guts of a winning club, has committed but a single error (though, as we will see, a costly error).

Which leaves the bullpen. In truth, the relievers have not done badly, not nearly as badly as local headlines suggest.

Dennis Lamp notched his second loss in the first Oakland outing by surrendering a two-run home run to Carney Lansford in the bottom of the eighth of another game the Jays led by a run as the frame began – another china cup smashed (late inning one-run leads on the road shatter easily), and another game in which Jim Clancy had nothing to show for several strong innings' work. Toronto's sports pages next morning declaimed in large type *Dennis the Menace* and *Bullpen kills Jays again*. Mm. Jabberwocky. (1) The runner on base whom Lansford drove in got there because Garcia booted a grounder (the error), and (2) he stayed there because the infield failed to turn a double play on the next hitter's grounder (Lamp is *supposed* to pitch grounders). (3) Earlier in the game the Jays had stranded two men on base in one inning and three in another. And (4) the pitch Lansford parked was a good sinker that he was lucky to have put wood on, much less smacked out; in the locker room afterward Lansford said he hadn't really meant to swing at the pitch – he had wanted to back off it – and he ended up sort of hacking at it like a man trying to drive a golf ball from the inside of a telephone booth. The plain fact is, sometimes you do your job right, and the other man beats you anyway. Lamp gets the rap for the loss in Seattle; he walked the winning run on base. And Roy Jackson had no business giving up back-to-back homers in Anaheim. Still, Lamp has done well now twice, Jimmy Key has thrown well twice, and Jackson bounced back from his loss to the Angels by pitching two-and-a-third nearly perfect innings to protect Leal's shutout in the second Oakland game. The bullpen has, to date at least, done its job more often than not.

Items:

• Tony Fernandez has again been X-rayed and diagnosed healed; he will report to Syracuse shortly. The only problem the Jays will have now is what to do with him when he is ready to come up. Alfredo Griffin is playing flawless shortstop.

• Joey McLaughlin is unhappy. He has yet to see action, and Cox and Gillick have repeated their misgivings about his exhibition work.

• Detroit has still not made a mistake. After seven games they are seven and oh. The Jays do not get a crack at them until June.

April 16
The Texas Rangers have not once been in post-season play and have played better than .500 ball in only six of their twenty-three seasons. They were managed in their first winning season, 1969 – they were still the new edition of the Washington Senators at the time; they did not move to Texas until 1972 – by a rookie skipper, name of Williams. It was Williams' only winning campaign as a manager. In his subsequent three years' tenure with the club their record dropped steadily to .432 to .396 to .351, at which point Williams said to hell with it and returned to his preferred avocation, fishing. It is arguable Williams never had a whole lot to work with in managing the Senators/Rangers, but it is also arguable Williams was a lot better trout angler than manager; running a ballclub was not his forte. Besides being a pretty good fisherman, he was also a pretty good hitter of pitched baseballs – maybe the best ever was; Williams' given name, of course, was Ted. It has been observed that good managers are usually marginal ballplayers who make up for what they lacked in natural gifts with a nurtured understanding of the game and how it works. Stars, on the other hand, do not seem to make very good teachers, usually having neither the ability nor patience to explain their craft to young ballplayers. This appears particularly true of star hitters whose skill often consists more of a kind of zen than of conscious application of principles of batting

mechanics. Story has it that, when Mickey Mantle was a rookie All-Star, he approached Williams at that year's festivities and, hoping to pick up a few tips, asked the great batsman about hitting. Williams discoursed for more than ten minutes. Mantle listened and nodded and returned to the other end of the dugout where the other Yankee All-Stars sat. One of them asked what Williams had said. "I don't know," said Mantle, mystified. "I don't know what the hell the man was talking about."

As in the case of most expansion franchises fallen on hard times, the Rangers' main problem has been unwise and inconsistent management. There is currently, though, a new regime in Texas, and last season the Rangers were the most improved team in the A.L. West, thirteen games ahead of their 1982 pace. Their strength was pitching, best in the league, and their weakness was offence, nearly worst in the league, and so over the winter they traded some pitching to bolster the offence. They are not likely to finish this year any better than the middle of the pack, but they have some good young ballplayers (George Wright, Gary Ward), some entertaining older ballplayers (Mickey Rivers, Charlie Hough), and at least one bona fide star ballplayer (Buddy Bell) and will be fun to watch.

The Jays' Texas stand was a three-game weekend set. Saturday's was a match best forgotten, the first of the season in which the Jays were out of it from inning one. Charlie Hough's knuckler zigged, bobbed, and darted for nine innings during which the Jays were unable to mount more than token offense. Jim Clancy's fastball was straight as an arrow, and Jim Gott, who relieved in the fifth, had no stuff at all. Ernie Whitt suffered through an uncharacteristically leadfooted afternoon during which he allowed two passed balls (he allowed only six all season in 1983), one of which permitted a run to score. Texas 6, Toronto 2.

The Friday and Sunday games, though, were dandies,

taut low-scoring affairs decided in the final innings. Friday's key hit was a two-out single in the top of the ninth by Dave Collins, who fought off a sequence of pitches until he found one he liked, which he poked through the infield to score Garcia. Garcia during the game was a regular one-man band, knocking three hits, stealing two bases, forcing two Texas errors, driving in the tying run in the fifth, then scoring the winner. Jimmy Key closed out the Rangers' ninth for a save. Toronto 3, Texas 2.

Sunday's game was deadly serious baseball in which Luis Leal and Ranger starter Dave Stewart battled grimly for nearly eight scoreless innings. Stewart, particularly, was helped by an impenetrable defence. With one out in the bottom of the eighth Wayne Tollenson whacked a hard hopper off Leal's glove; the ball bounced through to the outfield, a good hit but a lucky one. Tollenson then stole second as Leal worked Gary Ward for an infield groundout, and George Wright smacked a single to drive the run home. Cox replaced Leal with Lamp, who got the third out.

Stewart began the top of the ninth working quickly, throwing hard, and it did seem as though his colleagues' single run was all he would need to wrap matters up. Moseby knocked a tough grounder to rookie shortstop Curtis Wilkerson who made a pretty play. One down. Willie Upshaw stepped in, and Stewart offered a fast slider. Oops. Upshaw nailed it: tie game. Stewart perhaps might have paused to consider this new situation but did not. He came too quickly after Cliff Johnson, and his very first pitch was a hanging curve that dangled before Johnson like a fat pork chop. *Whack.* Downtown. Jays 2, Texas 1. Bell then knocked a double, and that was the end of Stewart. After eight fine innings he had come apart. Reliever Dave Tobik got some fielding help from Wilkerson to end the frame – Bell died on third – and now it was Texas's turn. *You've got to throw the ball over the goddamn plate and give the other man his chance.*

Lamp set the Rangers down one-two-three (F8, G1, G4),

and the Jays had won their road trip six games to four. They were also finally above .500 against another A.L. club, a moment for which they had waited a long time.

Standings, A.L. East, April 16

	W	L	PCT.	GB
Detroit	8	0	1.000	—
Toronto	6	4	.600	3
Cleveland	4	4	.500	4
New York	4	6	.400	5
Boston	3	6	.333	5½
Milwaukee	3	7	.300	6
Baltimore	2	6	.250	6

FIVE

Birds of a Different Feather

Extra bases and extra outs, that's what fundamentals are all about. You want to make the other team earn all four bases, and you don't want to give them any extra outs.
— Earl Weaver

It almost irritates other players. They'll ask you in August, "Don't you guys ever throw a ball away? Don't you ever miss a cutoff man?"
— Ken Singleton

April 17

The Jays have arrived in Toronto for their first homestand of the season, which they will open with a three-game set against the Orioles.

The Milwaukee Brewers, managed by Hugh Duffy and paced by slugging first sacker Honest John Anderson, won only forty-eight games and lost eighty-nine their first season; it was also their last season. The year was 1901, the first campaign of the new American League. That winter the franchise moved to St. Louis and became the Browns. The Brewers' modern namesakes did not arrive in Milwaukee for another sixty-nine years.

The St. Louis Browns had maybe the least distinguished history of any professional baseball club. They played better than break-even ball in only twelve of their fifty-two seasons and won but a single pennant, in 1944, during baseball's unsettled war years, and barely won it, closing ahead of the Tigers by just one game. They lost that autumn's World Series, four games to two, to the Cardinals, their tenants at St. Louis's Sportsman's Park. And while most franchises have left some enduring image etched in the game's history, even clubs whose records have been among the least auspicious (the Phils did have the Whiz Kids, and the Indians had their incomparable 1954 pitching staff), the Browns are remembered for almost nothing. Most current fans would be hard-pressed to name even a single member of the pennant-winning 1944 club.

The odd Hall of Famer did pass through St. Louis. Jesse Burkett, Eddie Plank, Rube Waddell, Jim Bottomley, and Satchel Paige were all Brownies at the tail ends of their careers; Heinie Manush and Goose Goslin each played a couple of years in St. Louis. But only two later denizens of Cooperstown were Browns through their finest seasons, shortstop Bobby Wallace (1902-1916), by all accounts the best infielder of his era, and first baseman George Sisler

(1915-1927), a gifted fielder and lifetime .340 hitter. Apart from these two, had there never been a St. Louis Browns, baseball would hardly have noticed.

In 1954 the Browns moved to Baltimore and became the Orioles, also a club name with a history; a franchise named the Baltimore Orioles had played in the A.L. in 1901 and 1902 before moving to New York to become the Highlanders, later the Yankees.* In their first half-dozen years, during which they never rose out of the second division, the new Orioles offered little reason to believe they were much improvement on their St. Louis forebears. But baseball is a patient business; under the surface of those mediocre late-fifties clubs Baltimore management was building one of the strongest franchises in the game's history. From 1960 until today, no team has won nearly as many games or finished nearly as consistently a pennant contender. By 1983 the Orioles had won three World Series, six pennants and, in the fifteen years since the leagues were halved, seven division titles. When they did not win, they were almost always close. In five other years they were less than three games out, and only twice, in 1962 and 1967, did they play sub-.500 ball.

The success of the Baltimore franchise has involved a baseball shibboleth old as the game: fundamentals. The club has had stars, flocks of them: MVP's Brooks Robinson, Frank Robinson, Boog Powell, Cal Ripken; Cy Young winners Mike Cuellar, Jim Palmer, Mike Flanagan, Steve Stone; the two finest fielding shortstops of their eras (heirs to Bobby Wallace), Luis Aparicio and Mark Belanger; the two most potent switch-hitting sluggers since Mickey

* There were also Baltimore Orioles in the old American Association (1882-91) and later in the National League in the 1890s. The latter club numbered on its roster within a few short years seven future Hall of Famers: Dan Brouthers, Hugh Jennings, Willie Keeler, Joe Kelley, and Joe McGinnity, who entered the Hall as players; and Wilbert Robinson and John McGraw, who entered as managers.

Mantle: Ken Singleton and Eddie Murray. But stars alone do not make a winning ballclub. The Orioles' success has been rooted in a simple principle: *do not beat yourself.*

It is not accidental that some of Baltimore's most consistent league-leading stats have involved not offence but defence; in the field the Orioles give away nothing. Oriole pitchers, for their part, are typically not overpowering fastballers or exponents of odd new stuff but pitchers who spot corners, change speeds, mix junk, throw strikes. Finally there has been the offence, an attack built around a rudimentary weapon: the home run, preferably the three-run home run. (The O's are not a club of whom it is said "They beat you a dozen different ways." They usually do not steal many bases and have not had much of a bunting game, and their club batting average is typically near the middle of the pack.) And it has not been only stars who have built Baltimore's record but also journeymen, the Elrod Hendricks, Terry Crowleys, Sammy Stewarts, Benny Ayalas, each of whom has had a particular job and has known the job. The Orioles field twenty-five-player ballclubs. It is also not accidental that Oriole locker rooms are usually cheerful places whose inhabitants seem to get on well together.

The Oriole system's most notable tactician was, of course, Earl Weaver, the club's manager for fifteen years (1968-1982) and a master of the game. Weaver's Oriole clubs played .595 ball. Not Cap Anson, John McGraw, Casey Stengel, Walter Alston – only Marse Joe McCarthy and Frank Selee had better managerial records. Yet the Orioles won their first World Series in 1966, before Weaver's arrival, and their most recent in 1983, after his departure. They will not be as strong a club without him, but the franchise remains, from its scouts through its minor league system to its front office, among baseball's soundest.

By the close of the 1983 season no club had, over the years, whipped the young Jays more mercilessly than the

Orioles. Toronto had played against Baltimore .303 ball. Other clubs had hit the Jays harder, pitched them better, but in respect to games won, the only stat which really matters, Baltimore had powdered them. (In one particular span, 1979 to 1982, the Jays had won nine games against the Orioles and lost thirty-seven.) And of all the Jays' losses to the O's the one that hurt most and maybe mattered more than all the others together was the game of August 24, 1983, probably the most memorable game the Jays played in their first seven seasons.

The Jays, as we saw, were bunched with the O's, Brewers, and Tigers at the top of the A.L. East, a game and a half off the pace, and had thumped the Orioles 9-3 in the previous night's match in which the usually slick-fielding Baltimores made three errors and surrendered four unearned runs in a single inning. No one knew at the time that the Orioles would go on to win the division, pennant and World Series in the manner of a bulldozer addressing a weed patch. They had played until then five months of streaky ball, winning and losing in baffling bunches. (Against the Jays they had lost three of four in Toronto in May, then won three of four in Baltimore in June.) The three-error inning the night before had been typical; the O's seemed headed for second place, maybe third. Perhaps only their fans, familiar with their club's ways and habits, guessed what might happen, knew it is at this moment of the season that the O's become most dangerous. Down the pennant stretch, through the last five or six weeks of the season, the Orioles more often than not have played at least .650 ball.

The Jay starter that night was Jim Clancy. Lloyd Moseby tripled and scored for the Jays in the third, but the Orioles answered with a run of their own a couple of outs later. In the fifth and eighth the Jays scratched out two more, which were still not answered by the bottom of the ninth. Clancy got an out, gave up a bunt single, then struck out Gary Roenicke, who had come in to pinch-hit for the O third baseman. Note the moment. In the course of the subsequent one and a half innings of baseball – the managerial strategies alone are worth a dissertation – the years of the upstart Jays and uncanny Orioles would turn around.

The next scheduled batter was reserve second baseman Lenn Sakata, one of the weaker hitters in the Oriole order. Oriole manager Joe Altobelli, Weaver's successor, would ordinarily have pinch-hit for Sakata here, but he had used up all his other infielders in earlier innings, so was forced to leave Sakata in place. Clancy was unable to nail down the elusive third out; he gave Sakata a base on balls.

Bobby Cox dispatched Clancy to the showers and turned the ball over to the Jays' only lefty, reliever Dave Geisel, to pitch to the left-hitting Oriole catcher, Joe Nolan. Cox reckoned Altobelli was now eight-balled because Altobelli had also used up his only other catcher and would be forced to leave Nolan in to face the Jay southpaw.

Altobelli demurred. He yanked Nolan and went for the win, sending to the plate Benny Ayala, one of the more dangerous pinch-hitters in the league. (Six weeks later Ayala tagged the single which knocked Steve Carlton out of the World Series.) Altobelli was playing for the three-run homer which would eliminate need for a catcher; the game would be over. Cox, looking ahead to the Orioles' on-deck batter, Al Bumbry, left Geisel in to face Ayala. (Cox knew that Ayala was the last rabbit left in Altobelli's hat. He had been the last player left on the Oriole bench who was not a pitcher, and so Altobelli could not pinch-hit for lefty Bumbry.)

Ayala did not hit the homer but did whack a single to drive in a run. Jays 3, O's 2. The Bullpen Massacre had begun. Bumbry, the man Geisel was supposed to get if he could not get Ayala, singled too, scoring Sakata. Tie game. Cox had seen enough of Geisel and went to the pen for righty Joey McLaughlin to face Oriole righty Dan Ford. McLaughlin whiffed him. Extra innings.

In spite of losing a two-run lead with two out in the bottom of the ninth, the Jays entered the tenth with some optimism. They had not lost an extra-inning game all season and had won nine. (The last extra-inning game they had lost, in fact, had been exactly one year to the day earlier in this very same Baltimore ballpark. Catcher Joe Nolan had cranked a grand slam home run off McLaughlin in the bottom of the tenth. There was an entrail here to be read. . . .) And with his pinch-hitting tactics in the ninth, Altobelli had blown his defensive wad. With no catcher, he was forced to put utilityman Sakata behind the plate, Sakata's first catching appearance since Little League. This left second base empty, so Altobelli put his leftfielder, John Lowenstein, here; Lowenstein had last played second base in 1975 when he was an Indian – a couple of innings' worth. Altobelli also had no third baseman and so was forced to leave Roenicke here, his major league debut at the position. This left Ayala, as undistinguished a fielder as he was distinguished a hitter, in leftfield.

The Jays' optimism was enhanced when Cliff Johnson slammed Oriole reliever Tim Stoddard's first pitch of the tenth deep past the left-centrefield fence. Jays 4, O's 3. Barry Bonnell then sliced a single, and managerial cogwheels cranked into action in both dugouts. Cox sent switch-hitter Dave Collins out to hit for Barfield against righty Stoddard, and Altobelli replaced Stoddard with his ace reliever, southpaw Tippy Martinez. The stage was now set for a sequence of events which, so far as anyone can recall, was unique in the annals of major league baseball.

The key was Sakata, an infielder suddenly turned catcher. Cox and the Jays reckoned they might test Sakata's arm to advantage, and Bonnell leaned away from first. Martinez picked him off. One out. The Jays got their base runner back when Collins drew a walk, and Collins, a base thief of established credentials, could surely get a jump on Sakata, yes? Maybe. The Jays never found out. Collins led off from first, and Martinez picked him off. Two outs. Willie Upshaw now cracked a single. He, too, leaned toward second. Martinez picked him off.

Amid baseball's voluminous statistical cargo one number not kept is runners picked off, and so the record is silent about whether three outs in an inning had ever previously been logged in this fashion. If it ever did happen, no one can remember when. After the game Lowenstein is said to have offered this explanation for what occurred: "Tippy looked around and saw Lenn catching and Gary at third and me at second, and the only guy he recognized was Eddie (Murray, at first), so he kept throwing the ball to him." More to the point, the Jays had suckered themselves into a critical tactical error. In their eagerness to exploit Sakata's thorough inexperience as a catcher, they had let the O's slip out of the inning without really pressing Altobelli's jerryrigged infield. Still, they went into the bottom of the tenth with a one-run lead.

It did not last a batter. Oriole shortstop Cal Ripken led off with a homer that departed the premises on roughly the same route as Johnson's. McLaughlin now pitched too carefully to Murray and walked him – not necessarily a mistake; Murray is one of the most lethal clutch hitters in the league. Lowenstein then grounded out to the right side, usefully; this advanced Murray to second. Cox directed McLaughlin to create a double-play situation by intentionally passing centrefielder John Shelby, then hooked McLaughlin for Randy Moffitt, a pitcher more likely to sucker a batter into hitting a ground ball. Roenicke, however, struck out. Still, even without the double play, Cox had Altobelli in a corner: now up, with two out, was the meekest bat in the Oriole order, Sakata, with utterly no one left on the bench to pinch-hit. Sakata stepped in. Moffitt pitched. Sakata slammed the ball past the leftfield fence for a three-run homer.

From those one and a half innings of notable baseball the Orioles went down the stretch at a .700 clip and won the division by six games. The Jays did not play badly after that, winning nineteen and losing seventeen, but their pennant race ended that night. During the next six days they would lose five more games in the final inning.

8/24/83: Orioles 7, Blue Jays 4

Toronto	ab	r	h	rbi		Baltimore	ab	r	h	rbi
Garcia, 2b	5	0	0	0		Bumbry, cf	4	0	1	2
Moseby, cf	4	1	2	0		Ford, rf	5	0	0	0
Iorg, 3b	4	1	2	1		Ripken, ss	5	1	1	1
Johnson, dh	4	1	1	1		Murray, 1b	3	1	0	0
Bonnell, lf	5	1	2	0		Lowenstein, lf-2b	5	0	0	0
Barfield, rf	4	0	2	0		Singleton, dh	1	0	1	0
Collins, rf	0	0	0	0		Shelby, dh	1	2	1	0
Upshaw, 1b	5	0	2	0		Dauer, 2b-3b	2	0	0	0
Martinez, c	3	0	0	1		Roenicke, 3b	2	0	0	0
Griffin, ss	4	0	0	0		Cruz, 3b	2	1	1	0
						Dwyer, ph	0	0	0	0
	38	4	11	3		Sakata, 2b-c	1	2	1	3
						Dempsey, c	2	0	0	0
						Nolan, c	1	0	0	0
						Ayala, lf	1	0	1	1
							35	7	7	7

```
Toronto      001 010   010  1____4    4 1 1 0
Baltimore    001 000   002  4____7    7 7 2
```

Two out when winning run scored.
E-Cruz 2. LOB-Toronto 9, Baltimore 8. 2B-Cruz. 3B-Moseby.
HR-Johnson, Ripken, Sakata. SB-Upshaw. SF-Iorg, Martinez,
Bumbry.

	IP	H	R	ER	BB	SO
Toronto						
Clancy	8 2/3	3	3	3	6	2
Geisel	0	2	0	0	0	0
McLaughlin (L)	2/3	1	3	3	2	1
Moffitt	1/3	1	1	1	0	1
Baltimore						
McGregor	9	8	3	2	2	2
Stoddard	0	2	1	1	0	0
T. Martinez (W)	1	1	0	0	1	0

Geisel pitched to 2 batters in the 9th. Stoddard pitched to 2
batters in the 10th. T-2:54. A-25, 882.

April 20

The Jays opened their homestand with three quick decisions against the Orioles. The set left Baltimore at two wins and ten losses, and first glance may suggest that, if the O's do not get on their horse soon, the Tigers – not to mention the Jays – may get too far in front for them to catch. Detroit has finally lost a game, to K.C., but has also won another and is eight games up on the hapless Orioles. But it is barely late April and will remain too soon to make any judgements about the course of the season at least until Baltimore and Detroit have had a go at each other in June. The Jays, for the moment, trail the Tigers by only a game and a half.

In their wins against Baltimore the Jays twice broke tied games in late innings, picking up where they left off last year, when only the Orioles and Mets had better records winning locked games in late frames. The Jays also had the majors' best come-from-behind record in 1983. The fact that they were one of the better late-inning ballclubs was obscured by the events of the week of their collapse.

In the first game of the set with the O's the score was 2-2 when Willie Upshaw, who had scored the tying run in the sixth, led off the bottom of the eighth with a first-pitch double; he then scored on a nice base hit by George Bell. *Sport* magazine, in its yearly baseball preview, under the rubric *You heard it here first...*, picked Upshaw as 1984's A.L. MVP, and he has done nothing so far to disabuse anyone of this possibility.* The game was won by Jimmy Key, his second, in relief of Doyle Alexander who looked sharp for all but one of his seven innings. Some fans on hand exhibited hair-trigger impatience with the Jays' pen in the top of the ninth when they got on Dennis Lamp, who had

---

* But he did not, in the end, have an MVP year. Though he remained a pivot of the Jay offence, slumps in June and September hurt his season.

come in to mop up for Key and who walked his first batter, Joe Nolan, on four pitches. Lamp was clearly pitching around Nolan, a portside batter who could hurt him with the long ball; there was a man on base. He preferred his chances against Rich Dauer, who hits right and does not have power, and who grounded out to end the game. The incident showed good judgement on Lamp's part and hasty judgement by some of the fans, who seemed not to fully grasp what was happening.

The occasion was, of course, the Jays' home opener, and apart from the momentary sourness directed at Lamp in the ninth, the mood was celebratory, like a holiday. Strangers packed together on transit buses bound for the park broke into animated conversation about the Jays, the club's chances this year, past opening days they had attended going right back to the days of the old minor league Maple Leafs. At the stadium the crowd, more than 35,000 strong, was particularly noisy and good humoured. The sounds of ball against leather and bat against ball and the first inning panorama of the home squad in crisp whites arrayed across the green of the field as the visiting leadoff hitter tosses away the tar rag and steps from the on-deck circle into the batter's box had returned for another season. The pitcher looks in, pumps into his wind-up, and delivers the first pitch, and the *game* has begun. Baseball was back, good reason for celebration.

On day two the crowd declined to 13,000. The quality of baseball declined as well. The game's outcome was never in doubt, Jays from inning one, which Garcia led off with a triple; he then scored on a single by Dave Collins. Against Dave Stieb the O's never had a chance, and Jim Palmer, a certain Hall of Famer but now seemingly near the end of his playing days, walked three, threw a wild pitch, and surrendered four runs in five innings. It is not fun to watch a once-gifted athlete struggle to avoid the inevitable arithmetic of passing years. Palmer is, however, one of the smartest pitchers in the game, and one does not want to write him off too quickly.* Former Jay Tom Underwood took the mound in Palmer's wake and promptly walked two more, then watched his leftfielder, Lowenstein, drop a fly ball; all three of these runners eventually scored – not Oriole baseball, and symptomatic of what has troubled the O's thus far this season. In their first eleven games of the season Baltimore pitchers have surrendered fifty-three bases on balls, twenty-three of whom scored. They have also thrown five wild pitches and have had their defence make ten errors in the field behind them, good for a dozen unearned runs.

For all that, the game did have a highlight, the base running of Dave Collins. After driving in Garcia in the first he immediately stole second, then stole third, but he was unable to score. In the fifth, however, he manufactured a run from pure speed, legging a single into a double, taking third on a fly to not-particularly-deep centre, and scoring on a fly to right. As he took the field for the sixth he sought to respond to the fans' applause with a stolid pokerface, but the smallest edge of a grin slipped through. He was having fun; he loves to run. Final score, 7-1.

The third game was Garth Iorg's. The Jays' affable expansion draftee and thirdsacker went four for four, including a triple, made a couple of sterling defensive plays, and drove in both Jay runs, the second in the bottom of the ninth, in a 2-1 match that, for a time, neither club seemed to want to win (l.o.b.'s: O's, nine; Jays, eight). The runner on base on both occasions was Willie Upshaw, whom Toronto fans are becoming accustomed to see in all the right places at the right times. Jim Clancy went nine and was not his sharpest – five walks – but finally logged a win, deserved after his ill-starred outings in Seattle and Oakland.

* Palmer, however, wrote himself off. A couple of weeks later he hung up his spikes and adjourned to the TV booth to do colour commentary.

64

The play of the game and possibly of the month was made by Jesse Barfield in the top of the eighth when Clancy seemed to be tiring. Clancy walked the leadoff Oriole, got an out, then walked Lowenstein and found himself facing Ken Singleton, who can pop a ball out of any park any time. The stage seemed set for a timely Baltimore three-run homer. And Singleton did get most of a Clancy fastball, but not quite all of it. The ball just failed to clear the fence in deep right centre where Barfield hauled it down with an acrobatic catch. Introductions were now in order – Mr. Lowenstein, meet Mr. Barfield. The Oriole base runner had gone most of the way to second, meaning to score if the ball hit off the wall, and now scampered like a frightened mouse back toward first. He did not scamper nearly fast enough. The Barfield cannon fired its round to Upshaw on a nearly perfectly flat trajectory. R.i.p. Lowenstein, double play. End of inning. End of Orioles.

The happiest Jay in the locker room afterward was Iorg who had, prior to the afternoon, been off to a horrible start with his bat this year. He answered one reporter, yes, it was nice to take three from the O's, and another reporter, yes, it was nice the Jays were finally winning after all those years of losing. A third reporter nodded in the direction of the Oriole locker room and said it was awfully quiet over there, and Iorg nodded and said nothing; a Jay since Day One, he knows what quiet locker rooms are like. A fourth reporter observed that it was the first scrum of writers around Iorg's locker this season, and Iorg nodded again and grinned. "I sure hope there's a bunch more of them, man."*

The Jays play a return set against the Orioles in two weeks in Baltimore.

---

* There were not a bunch more of them. Iorg had a difficult season. While his defensive work was consistently sharp – he was one of the best fielding thirdsackers in the league – he remained, at the plate, in a frustrating summer-long slump.

Items:
- Joey McLaughlin has still not seen action and has asked the Jays to play him or trade him.
- Willie Aikens' one-year suspension has been officially commuted. He will join the Jays May 16.
- Stan Clarke is throwing well down in Syracuse, but Bryan Clark still cannot find the strike zone.

April 27

The Orioles' malady appears to have been infectious. Of the remaining seven games of the homestand, the Jays dropped five and were lucky it was not six. In consequence, they have also dropped to third place, six and a half games behind the Tigers, who have now won sixteen and lost one (!), and a half a game behind the Indians, who are enjoying a flush of early-season good fortune.

With the Orioles' departure, Gene Autry's Anaheim gunslingers rode into the visitors' dugout for a few quick rounds of kick-the-carcass. In three days the Jays surrendered twenty-two earned runs, five unearned runs, and three ball games. Jay pitchers donated, among other things, fifteen bases on balls to the Angel cause. Five of these walkees later scored, and two others came to bat with duckies at all corners of the pond, hence were credited with r.b.i.'s without having lifted wood from shoulder. Jay fielders committed six official errors and a number of less scorable miscues. And the Jay offence, not to be left out of the proceedings' tenor, stranded twenty-six base runners). The matches commend themselves to no further critical exegesis, although two incidents worth recording did occur.

The first was Lloyd Moseby's first major league grand slam home run, which gave the Jays a 4-3 lead in the first game of the set, heroics which were unfortunately subsequently cancelled by Angel batsmen. The second was Jimmy Key's instruction in the lessons that (1) old guys can play this game too and (2), in the words of Catfish Hunter, "the sun don't shine on the same dog's ass all the time." The pedagogues were Profs. B. Grich, B. Boone, F. Lynn, D. DeCinces, and R. Jackson, precisely the same assemblage of baseball postgraduates whom Master Key had tightly collared in their own park two weeks ago. Key's first class, a brief one, was held shortly after Moseby's four-by-four when Grich and Boone tagged him for two-out doubles to lodge the game back at ground zero. Bobby Cox popped from the dugout and dismissed school posthaste. Class two, two days later, commenced when Cox dispatched Key to the mound in the sixth inning of a game locked at 3-3. Lynn singled, DeCinces homered, Jackson singled, and Grich homered; the Jays were abruptly four in the hole. On this occasion Cox did not hook Key, and the Angels' young pupil demonstrated grasp of his lesson by now shutting California down for two and two-thirds flawless innings – Cool Hand Key. It was his first major league loss.

Next came Seattle, with whom the Jays split a pair. Dave Stieb logged the winner only because the Mariners' hurling was, on balance, more inept than his own; he gave up eight hits, five walks, and four runs over seven innings. There was, however, rough justice in the outcome. Stieb has, in past, pitched some lovely ball games for the Jays, only to lose them because his offence chose these occasions to do uncanny impersonations of playdough. Clancy was more luckless in the next night's do, a rematch with Mike Moore, the young Mariner fastballer who muzzled the Jays in the season opener and now did so again.

Against Oakland the Jays split again, winning a game behind Luis Leal, who pitched a classy complete-game shutout, the club's only noteworthy mound job all week. Jesse Barfield lunged from his early-season batting torpor with a homer, two doubles, and four r.b.i.'s. The loss in the second game was less to the A's than to King Kong Kingman, who parked two, good for five runs. His victim was Jim Gott, losing his second game in as many starts.

Kingman's blasts had that particular timbre (*crack*) that

leaves utterly no doubt where the ball will settle from the moment orb meets bat – uh-oh homers; hearing that sound, all the unhappy pitcher can do is mutter, "Uh-oh." Dave Kingman is a curious animal, like one of those dinosaurs which is all massive megatoothed jaw: tiny brain, bandy legs, puny claws, a helpless critter but for that terrifying mouth. Kingman cannot field, cannot hit for average, does not run the bases very well, strikes out more often than nearly anyone who has ever hefted a bat. But every now and then he blunders into a Brobdingnagian home-run tear of the type that leaves opposing pitchers wondering why they did not consider an alternate career, perhaps muffler repair. The Mets tried for years to figure out something to do with the man and concluded nothing could be done; homers or not, he was one of the club's main weak links. Oakland manager Steve Boros decided during the spring, more or less on a winger, to give Kingman a shot at d.h., the one position on a ballfield for which he is suited, and so far this spring Kong leads the A.L. in homers and ribbies. He is, however, notorious for his streaks, and the season has months to go; if he does keep it up, Boros looks like a genius.*

The Jays also whacked four homers during the game, two by W. Upshaw and three back-to-back, but all were solos, yielding a bare four runs. The most remarkable homer of the day was, however, none of the above but a ninth-inning shot by Rickey Henderson, a rope that went deep, *deep* into Exhibition Stadium's leftfield stands, above the entry ramps. Dave Collins, who was in left for the Jays, did not twitch an eyebrow, went on staring in at home plate as though frozen at the moment of the pitch, and the crowd sat in mildly stunned silence. Henderson, better known for

---

* Kingman did have a pretty good year, knocking thirty-five homers, driving in 118 runs, and batting .268. Boros, however, was not around to accept plaudits; after his club's mediocre start, he was fired in May by an unhappy Oakland front office.

his base-running exploits, is said to possess "sneaky power." Damn sure does.

Item:

• Joey McLaughlin finally pitched this week, three mop-up assignments in games the Jays were losing, and gave up a few hits and a walk but no runs in five innings' work.

May 7

Ten days, eight games, seven digits in the Jays' win column. Whatever condition they contracted from the Orioles lasted only a week.

During a lightning road trip to K.C., Jay pitchers, mainly Alexander and Stieb, allowed the Royals no runs in two games – back-to-back shutouts. A third scheduled match was a rainout, and the Jays returned to Toronto for a three-game set with Texas and won two. During those two the Rangers seemed afflicted with a peculiar sort of amnesia, as though they had nearly entirely forgotten the meaning and purpose of the small round white object which kept pressing itself into their possession. They committed, in the two games, seven errors, threw five wild pitches, allowed two passed balls, and surrendered ten walks, all of which the Jays cheerfully exploited.

The game the Jays lost was a nasty one. Danny Darwin and Doyle Alexander pitched their hearts out for eight innings, and the ninth frame opened with Toronto sitting on a powderkeg 1-0 lead. Alexander then provided the tinder and Jimmy Key the spark for a four-run Texas rally, and the night ended 4-1 Rangers, another game to remember come autumn when the race for the flag may be a matter of fractions.

Texas departed, and K.C. moved in, returning Toronto's visit the previous weekend. The Jays seem to have the Royals' number this season,* albeit the Royals minus

* In the season's second half, it was the Royals who had the Jays' number.

George Brett, benched several weeks with a knee injury, and Willie Wilson, suspended by the Commissioner's office under the same terms as Willie Aikens. Again they swept a series from K.C., this time three games to none, and twice more broke tied games in the final inning. (The bulk of Jay games so far this year seems to have been decided in the last couple of frames.) In one of the squeakers Alfredo Griffin dragged a bunt down the first-base line with two out in the bottom of the tenth and beat it out as George Bell scored from third; Dave Stieb pitched all ten innings for his fifth win against no losses. And in the other Cliff Johnson whacked an opposite field single to drive in Jesse Barfield, who had doubled, in the bottom of the ninth. Griffin's bunt, particularly, was a thriller – Alfredo legging it down the line and crossing the bag an instant before the throw arrived, at which point the crowd did not immediately applaud but first exhaled, nearly all 16,000 of them, making a kind of loud hissing noise; *then* they applauded.

The third win against K.C. was a 10-1 laugher, four more r.b.i.'s for Barfield. Jim Gott pitched seven strong innings, his first good start of the season, after he was slowed in April by flu. The main question about Gott is not whether he can pitch effectively – he can – but whether he can do so durably. He was yanked by the fifth inning in fourteen of his thirty starts last season but also pitched four complete-game wins in which he yielded only five runs. His consistency this year will bear watching.

And so the Jays arrive in Baltimore having won nine of twelve. Since their drubbing in Toronto, however, the O's have been playing sound ball too and have also won nine of twelve, moving into third place behind the Jays and Tigers. It is only early May, and the pennant race is already taking shape.

May 9
Rain has delayed the Jays' Baltimore series; meanwhile the front office has done some tinkering. Geno Petralli is gone,

sold to a Cleveland farm club. In return the Indians have agreed not to reclaim Kelly Gruber if the Jays send him to Syracuse. Petralli's spot on the roster has been taken by Rick Leach, an outfielder cut by the Tigers this spring after five years' rattling around their organization. The Jays signed him to Syracuse in April, he has been hitting well there, and Cox says he will use him as a reserve fielder and leftside pinch hitter. Gruber's e.t.d. for Syracuse is next week, when Willie Aikens' suspension ends. And because Leach is an outfielder, the Jays are free to return Mitch Webster to the minors when Tony Fernandez comes up.

May 11

Put these two clubs together, and it is likely something memorable will happen. In Toronto two weeks ago it was the Barfield d.p., which knocked the stuffing from the Orioles' effort to stave off a Jay sweep. In Baltimore this week it was a mucked-up fielding play, which underlined a lesson clubs around the A.L. have been learning for a couple of decades now: you don't give the O's four-out innings.

The first game of the set was unremarkable, a flat Oriole win – to be expected, one supposes, given the law of averages. The O's smacked around Jim Clancy and Jim Acker for six runs and ten hits in five innings.

It was in the second game that the notable play occurred. The Jays bunched some hits for three runs in the early going, and Doyle Alexander pitched scoreless ball through five. Cal Ripken whacked a homer in the sixth, and Oriole third baseman Wayne Gross hit another in the seventh, but the Jays still led 3-2 after seven and a half. Dennis Lamp, who had replaced Alexander, got an out, then pitched with extraordinary care to Eddie Murray and walked him on four pitches, at which point Bobby Cox popped from the dugout and hooked Lamp for Jimmy Key to pitch to John Lowenstein.

It was an interesting decision. (1) Although Lowenstein is

a lefty, Lamp pitches the double-play ball, and the Os'
Memorial Stadium has thick natural grass, the ideal double-
play surface. Lowenstein, on the other hand, has grounded
into only eight double plays in the past two seasons. (2)
Lamp did seem in control. All of his pitches to Murray had
been low and tight on the strike zone. They were not, on the
other hand, *in* the strike zone. (3) Altobelli had only to hit
Benny Ayala for Lowenstein to take away Key's left-left
advantage, precisely what he did, and Ayala had been
pinch-hitting thus far in the season at a rate of .333.

Hence, it was an arguable move, and Cox's choice was
vindicated, in the end, by events: Key whiffed Ayala on a
pitch on which Murray was running, creating the chance
for an inning-ending double play. Murray, hung out to dry
between first and second, was trapped in a rundown. But
the Jays failed in their *fundamentals*. In the course of the
rundown they made two small mistakes, one by Garcia of
timing, one by Upshaw on a throw. The throw left Griffin
scrambling for the ball and swiping low at Murray, who
tried to sidesaddle past him. In slow-motion replays it is
impossible to tell whether Griffin did tag Murray. He later
said he did, but the umpire said he did not. Trouble was,
fooled by the Jays' faulty mechanics, the ump was out of
position, behind Murray, on the play. Tricky. Had the Jays
turned the rundown without miscue, Murray was a goner,
but now, given an extra out, the O's flattened Key like
a flounder. Ken Singleton, Todd Cruz, and Lenn Sakata
singled, Floyd Rayford homered, and when the Jays' finally
notched the fourth out, they were down 7-3. They rolled
over in the top of the ninth.

The third game of the set was a pretty good ball game.
Dave Stieb walked six, but none of them hurt him, particularly thanks to some inspired fielding by Garth Iorg, who
made improbable plays to start two d.p.'s and end Oriole
threats. By the bottom of the eighth the Jays were up 3-0.
(Two of the runs had come on Griffin's first homer of the
year, dropped just inside Memorial Stadium's short leftfield

pole.) The O's then countered for three runs with four singles and a walk. Again, Dennis Lamp had worked some critical batters for grounders but to no avail: the Oriole hits that drove in the runs were both hoppers through the infield. Damaso Garcia was arguably out of position on one of them, or the Jays might have turned a rally-killing double play. No one scored in the ninth, and the game went into the tenth tied three-all. In the frame's top the O's notched two outs, at which point Willie Upshaw, right time, right place, nailed a homer to deep left-centre. The O's came up, and Roy Jackson struck out Ripken, pitched around Murray, and struck out Sakata. Ayala then cracked a line drive snared by Iorg, his third fielding gem of the evening. Game to Jays, set to Orioles.

The Tigers, since we last observed them, have won nine and lost three for an overall record of twenty-five and four, matching the modern major league record for best start by a club in a season. The mark was set by the Dodgers, then of Brooklyn, in 1955, the Boys of Summer, who went on to clinch the flag in early September and win it by thirteen and a half games. If someone does not cool the Tigers off soon, there may be no pennant race at all in the A.L. East this year.

Standings, A.L. East, May 11

	W	L	PCT.	GB
Detroit	25	4	.862	—
Toronto	19	12	.613	7
Baltimore	16	15	.516	10
Milwaukee	13	15	.464	11½
Boston	13	17	.433	12½
New York	12	17	.414	13
Cleveland	11	16	.408	13

SIX

Tiger by the Tail

The Tigers are playing pretty good ball.
— Jesse Barfield

It ain't over 'til it's over.
— Yogi Berra

May 24

The Jays have been on a hot streak. Since leaving Baltimore they have played ten games and won eight. They have also dropped another game behind the improbable Tigers and are now eight out. It was said of the woebegone Phils of the 1920s, "On a clear day they can see seventh place." The Jays are having similar trouble seeing the backs of Detroit. And the Orioles are a remote thirteen and a half games off the pace.

The Tigers are playing .875 ball, not astonishing yet (the season is only a quarter gone), but nearly so. In their adventures they have set records (1) for the fastest start after forty games by a modern major league club and (2) for consecutive games won by an A.L. club on the road (seventeen, an arcane but noteworthy stat; the old mark, sixteen, was set by the 1912 Washington Senators). For the record, the hottest spring ball in the past ten seasons was played by the 1977 Dodgers who, at forty games, were clipping along at .750; they won their division that year by ten games. (In a study of quick starts the Dodgers pop up a lot. Their pattern in their winning years is often to run in front by June 1, then tough it out until autumn. This is interesting because the Dodgers in recent years have been the dominant club in the N.L. as the Orioles have in the A.L.; they have played in ten World Series since 1955 and won five of them. Their seasonal pattern, however, is quite different than that of the O's, who are typically cold in spring and red-hot in September.)

One knows the Tigers will stumble. Baseball, like weather, has relentless arithmetic. The thermometer may do something weird for a couple of days, but by season's end it averages out. You may wager your mortgage the Tigers will not be playing .875 ball come October or even July. But how far can they stumble? If they play only .500 ball from now until fall, they will win ninety-six games, and they need play only .525 ball to tally the ninety-nine games it has taken, on average, to win the A.L. East.

The question *how* have the Tigers been winning has a superficial answer and a more difficult answer. The superficial answer is found in the papers day by day – box scores, club stats, player averages. The Ti's lead the majors in hitting at .298 (the Jays are a distant second at .282) and pitching, with a staff e.r.a. of 2.66 (the Phils are a distant second at 2.89). They seem to have no conspicuous statistical shortcomings and are scoring a lot of runs in early innings, blowing clubs out while the crowd is still on its first beer. But stats only describe; they don't much help understand a club. To understand, one needs to follow a club game by game, absorb patterns for which box scores don't account, a nearly impossible long-distance exercise. The Tigers have been on network TV only a couple of times – although one of these appearances was particularly instructive inasmuch as it was the occasion of a no-hitter pitched by Detroit's staff ace, Jack Morris. While the Tigers' radio broadcasts do, after dark, often reach Toronto, the Jays are usually playing, too, and it is hard to follow two ball games at once. And so, in spite of the mass of baseball bookkeeping at hand, the Tigers remain largely a mystery.

One area in which box scores and stats are especially uninformative is defence. Box scores in the old days were not hugely more helpful in this respect but at least did record putouts, showing, for example, whether the bulk of a club's outs were made by the infield or outfield, useful in understanding pitching, and the names of players involved in d.p.'s. In modern box scores defence, much less amenable to easy statistical description than offence or pitching, is left mostly a cipher. With reference to the Tigers, it is hard to get a good grasp of their game without a good impression of the play afield of their fine middle infield tandem, Alan Trammell and Lou Whitaker, or their All-Star backstop, Lance Parrish, and this kind of impression comes only with repeated observation.

The fact that one does not have as good a picture of these Tigers as one might like points up an interesting feature of the club: like the Jays, they are pretty much a bunch of nobodies outside their hometown – apart from Morris, Parrish, Trammell, and Whitaker another Who-are-these-guys? puzzle. One knows about them one-by-one – John Grubb is a good fielder with some power; Kirk Gibson is 220 pounds of trouble looking for a place to happen; rookie Barbaro Garbey seems to know how to hit; Dave Bergman is a glove wizard – but what are they like as a club? At their current pace they will not be nobodies long.

If anyone is going to take a hunk out of the Tigers so the Jays and Orioles can get back in this thing, it may have to be the Jays and O's themselves. All three clubs have played the bulk of their games thus far against West Division teams; the Jays, for instance, have played only seven of forty games against East clubs. The first serious round of intradivisional play commences June 1, when the Tigers begin fourteen matches in thirteen days against their feathered rivals, paired sets of home-and-away series. If the Tabs emerge from this *cours d'longball* with Toronto and Baltimore un-scathed, the Jays and O's may be playing catch-up all summer.

The Jays have been playing interesting ball, not devastating ball but pretty good box office. Six of their eight recent wins have been by a single run, and in five of the eight they have played catch-up, dropping behind early and winning late, usually in their last at-bats. And when they have not played catch-up, they have still offered late-inning drama. In one game, case in point, they carried a 4-1 lead against Minnesota into the eighth inning, but the Twins managed with Jay help to load the sacks in both that and the ninth frames. The day's business was not done until the final fragile out. Jay fans would probably rather be spared this sort of excitement in favour of nice dull three-up, three-down opposition-inning boredom, but the Jays seem to prefer high-wire fandangos with no net. When you leave the park after one of these squeakers, you know you have been to a ball game.

This is a winning pattern which seems to speak of timely hitting but speaks more pointedly of sound pitching. Regard the scores of seven of the eight Jay wins: 5-2, 3-2, 4-3, 1-0, 3-2, 3-2, 4-1. Jay hurlers have been keeping the club in the game, permitting the offence, at whatever eleventh-hour moment it anoints on a given occasion, to stir from its slumber. While the Jays have been bagging a lot of base hits and are second in the league in hitting, they are a remote fifth in runs scored; and they have not been hitting a lot of homers nor sufficiently bunching the hits they do get. Hence, they are accumulating a lot of l.o.b.'s, which stat, were they not winning, would weigh around their necks like a four-ton millstone. But thanks to the mound staff's doggedness, they are winning.

Pitching was especially the story in a pip of a four-game set against the White Sox in which a grand total of sixteen runs, eight by each club, were scored – meagre pickings. LaMarr Hoyt, Britt Burns, Rick Dotson, and Tom Seaver worked in the games for the Sox, a tough rotation when they have their stuff, and they did. But the committees of Jays Bobby Cox sent to the mound (he is averaging lately about three pitchers a game) proved the Palehose' match. The Jays won three and lost one; the loss was a 3-0 shutout by Dotson, Dave Stieb's first defeat of the season. The set's highlight was a match in which Seaver held the Jays to a single run but four Jays held the Sox to none, yielding an impeccable 1-0 score.

On the subject of pitching, it appears a stopper may have emerged, at least for the time, from Toronto's pen. Roy Lee Jackson has, at this date, an e.r.a. of 1.17, has stranded nineteen of the twenty runners on base when he has come into games, and in the past ten days has logged three wins – the yield of Jay hitters' late-inning heroics – for a record of five and one and two saves. (The loss was the April game against California in which he grooved successive pitches to Reggie Jackson and Doug DeCinces.) On the mound Jackson works slowly, deliberately, unflappably, often seeming like he is not entirely sure how he found himself wearing this outfit and throwing this ball but, what the hell, as long as he's here, he'll do what he can. Beneath this demeanor is a hard competitor, and lately Jackson has been painting Rembrandts out there.

The expected roster changes have occurred. Willie Aikens and Tony Fernandez are up, Kelly Gruber and Mitch Webster are down. Aikens, who had expressed misgivings about how fans might react to a convicted narcotics offender on the club, was greeted in his first Exhibition Stadium at-bat by loud and sustained applause. So much for bygones. In that first at-bat Aikens popped up, but in his second a.b. a couple of innings later, when he was cheered again, he slammed a loud double. When he arrived at the plate for his third at-bat, there was a third thunderous ovation. This was not, however, so much for Aikens as for a scoreboard announcement that the Edmonton Oilers were leading the Islanders in a Stanley Cup game, goal by Gretzky. Aikens, who would probably not know an Edmonton Oiler if one whacked him in the backside, seemed a little nonplussed.

Shortly after Fernandez's arrival Bobby Cox bit an ugly bullet and benched Alfredo Griffin for one end of a doubleheader. Griffin did appear in the game as a pinch runner, but this was, under the rules, insufficient to sustain his run of consecutive games, which stopped at 392. (Never mind that, in his brief appearance, Griffin scored the game's winning run – driven in, coincidently, by Fernandez.) As much as the Iron Man is a favourite of the fans and of his teammates and Cox, and as much as one will miss the streak now that it is over, Cox's move was hard to argue with. The streak was a small but constant distraction in what is already a tough pennant race. And now there is no longer question that Cox is playing Griffin for the sake of the streak; he is playing him because he is a good ball-player.

Griffin has his detractors. Bill James, for example, wrote in his *Abstract* this spring, "What are they waiting for? Who is Alfredo Griffin to keep anybody waiting?", meaning, of course, Fernandez, who may be every bit as good as his billing. Although Fernandez has yet to notch a hit, his glove-work and base running are dazzling; and the hitting, one senses, will come in time.

James does interesting things with numbers, but this is another case in which stats tell only a superficial story. James has simply not seen Griffin play enough ball –not seen him squeeze an extra base out of an unlikely situation (Griffin is one of the smartest base runners around) or execute one of the improbable heads-up plays that charac-terize his defensive work (he is also a pretty smart infielder). There are a lot of the little pieces of Griffin's game that do not show up in box scores or stats.

Still, whatever the solution to the Griffin/Fernandez di-lemma, it is not to leave Fernandez idle on the bench; he will see more play now. Among Cox's strengths as a skipper is effective use of his whole squad; he gives even Willie Upshaw and Lloyd Moseby the odd day off. Griffin was not, it may be noted, closing in on any all-time marks with his streak. The record for consecutive games played almost entirely at shortstop is held by Everett Scott who played for the Red Sox and Yanks in the 1910s and 1920s: 1,307. Joe Sewell, of the 1920s Indians, also played more than a thou-sand straight games almost all at shortstop; Sewell is, of course, best known as the hardest batter to strike out in the history of baseball: 114 K's in more than 7,000 at-bats.

So the bad news is that the streak is over; the good news is that Griffin, a class act, is unlikely to let this put him off his game.

There has been another roster change, too, which, one

supposes, was also expected. Joey McLaughlin is gone, replaced by Bryan Clark, who, according to reports, had turned it around in Syracuse.

McLaughlin's first outing as a Jay was in April 1980 in a game in which Dave Lemanczyk needed relief help to wrap up his season's first win; Jerry Garvin was unequal to the task. The opposing club was Cleveland. The Jays had a two-run lead on an Otto Velez homer. Garvin opened the bottom of the eighth by tendering an Indian a base on balls. The next batter was the Tribe's d.h., a hitter who could tie the game with a stroke and who, in past, had carved Garvin into little pieces, one Cliff Johnson. Johnson's long-ball record against Garvin was hellacious; it included one game in which Johnson, then a Yankee, tagged his habitual victim for three home runs, among them two in one inning. Bobby Mattick yanked Garvin and sent out McLaughlin, and McLaughlin fanned Johnson quickly and recorded the five remaining Indian outs without allowing a base runner. In his second Jay outing, against the Royals three days later, McLaughlin was less fortunate, hung with a loss after three unearned runs scored. But two days later against Milwaukee, McLaughlin pitched four runless innings and earned a win that lodged Toronto in first place in the A.L. East, where they remained nearly two weeks, the club's strongest start yet.

McLaughlin's contributions were noteworthy on three other occasions in Jay history. Late in 1981, when the Jays were struggling to turn in a respectable second half after a horrible season's start, McLaughlin logged six saves and a 0.63 e.r.a. during the final month. In mid-1982 McLaughlin recorded six consecutive relief wins in which he allowed only one earned run and permitted no inherited base runners to score. And in spring 1983, when the Jays startled baseball by moving into pennant contention, McLaughlin came into a game against Baltimore May 20 with the bases loaded and two out in the ninth and whiffed John Lowenstein for the save. On May 24 he pitched two scoreless innings against the Tigers, saving the game that put the Jays in first place. They slipped to second a few days later but were back in first May 30 after another game against Detroit in which McLaughlin logged the win.

McLaughlin had rough moments, too, when his stuff just hung there and was deposited by hostile batsmen in the nether reaches of the bleachers. In 1983 he surrendered eleven home runs in sixty-five innings pitched. And there were times when he could not find the plate. In a game against the Yankees in June 1982, he accomplished the unique indistinction of twice walking the same batter on four pitches to drive in the go-ahead run. He entered the game, which was tied, in the eleventh inning in relief of Roy Jackson, who had left the bags full, and promptly walked – one ball, two balls, three balls, four balls – Andre Robertson, not a strong hitter, to put the Yanks up by one. The Jays retied the score in the frame's bottom, but in the thirteenth McLaughlin, with the aid of an errant Jay infielder, loaded the bases again. Again Robertson came to bat, and again McLaughlin walked him on four economical pitches, this time to drive in the run that turned out to be the winner. The book on McLaughlin was that he was inconsistent, too often beaten not by the other team but by his own mistakes. The book said he wasn't aggressive enough, lacked the instinct for the jugular that sorts out the good relief pitchers.

McLaughlin's roughest moment was late last season. It started in that ill-starred game in Baltimore August 24. McLaughlin did not surrender the run which tied the game in the ninth (Dave Geisel did that) or Lenn Sakata's three-run homer which won it (Randy Moffitt did that). But he had allowed Cal Ripken's game-tying shot in the tenth, and one of the runners Sakata drove in was his (the other was Bobby Cox's, an intentional walk). In the end, the loss was his. In Detroit a few nights later he came into a game which the Jays led 3-1 with two out in the bottom of the ninth and a runner, walked by Geisel, on first. He allowed Rick Leach a single, Chet Lemon followed with an ugly homer, and McLaughlin was collared with another nightmare loss. It was the whole bullpen that crumbled that week, but McLaughlin came to symbolize the collapse in the opinions of enough Jay fans and press corps followers to matter. Maybe they sensed, the way a mob does, vulnerability. McLaughlin became a scapegoat, and in September it got so bad that he had to ask his wife not to come to the park to watch him work. (Crowd psychology is a funny thing. Only a minority of fans got on McLaughlin's case, but their voices seemed somehow to become the only ones that mattered.)

This spring other voices were heard. The loudmouths still took their kick at the can now and then but were outnumbered by fans who gave McLaughlin friendly waves and shouts of encouragement as he warmed up in the bullpen, people who seemed to want to make up for what McLaughlin had been put through last autumn. McLaughlin himself looked forward to a fresh start in 1984, but the year turned sour quickly. Cox and Gillick were, in spite of his good numbers in Florida, unhappy with his work, and he remained idle through most of April. After a request that the Jays play him or trade him (the club had already unsuccessfully tried to trade him), Cox did use him on some inconsequential occasions but never in the clutch. And then in Cleveland May 12, in the same park in which he had logged his first save as a Jay four years earlier, his chance finally came.

Leal was knocked out, Acker was ineffectual, Jimmy Key pulled a muscle, and the game, tied 3-3, became McLaughlin's to win or lose. He allowed his first hitter a run-scoring single (the runner was Acker's), walked his second, and was charged with an error when he tried to pick off a runner. Rance Mulliniks then threw a ball away, allowing another run to score, and before the inning ended McLaughlin had walked home a third run. In the next inning he got an out but then walked two batters; both scored on a double off the centrefield wall. By next morning he was no longer a Blue Jay, released outright. His departure completes the club's purge of the relievers who were battered that night in Baltimore last August: Moffitt, Geisel, McLaughlin; all gone.

Curiously, McLaughlin seemed to sense that the script was already written even as he took the Cleveland mound May 12. Ernie Whitt, who caught him, said afterward that McLaughlin had seemed depressed, like his heart wasn't really in the game. He has since been signed to a minor league contract with the Texas Rangers, a chance for a new beginning in a new city.

June 4

The Tigers are mortal after all. They have played nine games in ten days, lost six, and are no longer the stuff of history; they cannot now match the 1946 Red Sox' mark of forty-one wins in their first fifty games or the 1928 and 1939 Yanks' mark of forty out of fifty. And the Ti's are now nearly within shooting distance of the irrepressible Blue Jays, who have not similarly stumbled and with whom they begin a four-game set tonight.

The Tabs were first leashed by the Mariners, who swept a three-game series from Detroit in the Kingdome. None of the scores was even close – 7-3, 9-5, 6-1. The Ti's next won two of three from the A's in Oakland but then lost two of three to the Orioles in Detroit. The Tigers blew the O's out 14-2 in the first match of the set, but Baltimore rebounded in game two to thump Jack Morris 5-0; the shutout was pitched by young Oriole hurler Storm Davis. And so the series came down to game three, a 2-1 squeaker in which the decisive run scored when the Ti's gave the O's a four-out inning. The Orioles are now, in spite of their horrible start, slightly ahead of their pace last year when they won the whole cookie, and their press lately has been curious. Most clubs at nine and a half out would get barely nodding notice, but now that the Tigers are faltering, the O's ink has started to suggest that it may be Detroit, not Baltimore, who is the underdog in this race. Detroit will have an opportunity to douse this sort of sentiment in a four-game set in Baltimore in a few days' time.

The Tigers' gaffes have meant, among other things, they are no longer baseball's hottest club. This distinction is now the tenacious Blue Jays', who have won sixteen of their past twenty games. While the Tigers were suffering the indignities of Seattle, the Jays were at home stomping the Indians silly, four games to none. Again, pitching and defence were the story. Dave Stieb, Doyle Alexander, Luis Leal, and the Jay fielders held Cleveland to a bare run apiece in three of the matches. Matters would not, of course, have been complete without a couple of one-run ball games marked by late-inning dramatics. The Jays waited in one game until the Indians had scored a run in the top of the seventh to reply with two runs in the frame's bottom; in another they waited until the bottom of the ninth to catch up and pull ahead.

After Cleveland's departure the Jays journeyed to Chicago to return the White Sox' visit and were pasted 8-1 in the first game of two. The Sox' victim was Jim Clancy, blown away in a six-run eighth inning. The moral of the story may be that, if you persist in playing late-inning craps, you will sooner or later come acropper. LaMarr Hoyt, who hurled the game for the Sox, shut the Jays down cold; their only run was unearned.

The following night the two clubs returned to the pattern of games played in Toronto last week, tense, nearly flawless zen baseball. Stieb and Britt Burns both came to pitch, but the advantage leaned slightly to Stieb after the Jays managed to bunch some singles and scrape out a couple of early runs. The game went into the bottom of the ninth 2-0, but Stieb then donated Chicago a base on balls – again the Jays were uncontent to simply remove the cake from the oven without stumbling, bobbling it, nearly splattering it all over the kitchen before regaining composure. Stieb got an out, but Ron Kittle, a young slugger who was the A.L.'s rookie of the year last season, then drove a hanging slider deep to the gap in left centre. Only adroit play by Lloyd Moseby, first snaring the ball before it reached the wall, then rifling a peg to the infield that sent the Sox base runners panicking for the nearest bag, prevented a run from scoring and stopped Kittle from legging out a triple. Cox replaced Stieb with Jimmy Key, who notched the second out on a groundout. The runner from third, however, scored on the play, so Moseby's work a moment earlier may have been a game-saver. Key got the third out, and it was over: Jays 2, Sox 1; Jay fans, a few more grey hairs.

No one is surprised any more when Moseby makes this sort of play. He has blossomed in two years from a promising but still raw kid into one of the A.L.'s star centrefielders. The Jay front office selected Moseby in the first round of the 1978 amateur draft – Toronto chose second that year – in anticipation of such a blooming. Moseby's emergence did, however, need patience.

He took over centrefield for the Jays in mid-1980 at the tender age of twenty-one after the incumbent, Rick Bosetti, fractured an elbow and was lost for the season. Moseby had played in the minors barely more than two years – a year with Medicine Hat in the Pioneer League, a year in the Florida Instructional League, a few dozen games at Syracuse – a fairly meteoric rise for a young ballplayer. With the Jays that season he fielded awkwardly and, in his first experience with major league pitching, hit .229, about a hundred points off his minor league average. Over the next couple of years his stats did not improve much, but he was learning – learning what a kid usually learns in the minors, a luxury ballplayers on expansion clubs have not always enjoyed. Though he batted only .233 and .236 those years, he was becoming a more skilled situational hitter (the arrival of Cito Gaston helped); and his fielding was improving constantly.

Last year Moseby's game came together. Bobby Cox in-

dicated in spring that school was out, Moseby would platoon until he was able to carry centrefield, by major league
specs., on his own. No more coddling. Moseby, an intensely
proud young man, responded by playing the best ball of
his life, and his gifts are such that, when he is playing good
ball, not many players are in his class. He did not platoon
long. Thus far this year he is batting only .284, down a
notch from last season's .315; but his fifty-five hits in fifty
games have included eight doubles, eight triples (in which
department he leads the league), and nine home runs. He
is near the top of the league in total bases, has stolen thirteen bases, and has driven in thirty-three runs and scored
thirty-five, both Jay club highs.

Moseby is not entirely surprised by his offensive accom-
plishments – he knows he can hit and knows he can run –
and the side of his game of which he is proudest is his
defence. It was here he worked hardest, drilling, studying,
mastering his job. His goal is a Gold Glove, and he no
doubt will have one, maybe as soon as this year. He leads
the league in putouts and chances accepted by a centrefielder. No one cuts off the gaps more quickly and consistently. And his arm is strong, accurate, and – word has
gotten around – respected. If he is not in centrefield when
the A.L. All-Stars take the field in Candlestick Park next
month, it will be partly because he does not play in a U.S.
media centre, has not been around long enough, has not
played on a World Series club; the fans, who do the voting,
simply do not know him well enough yet. In time, they will.
During the past winter the Jays signed Moseby to a fat
long-term contract, acknowledging that his future is, in
significant part, the future of the franchise.

The Jays returned home from Chicago for a strange three-
game set with the Yanks. The first match was a Jay blowout,
10-2. The game was Doyle Alexander's first outing against
New York since that club cut him last year with a perfunc-

tory announcement he no longer "had it." Alexander issued a personal dispatch to George Steinbrenner on the topic of whether he any longer "had it" by baffling the Bombers for eight shutout innings – the two runs the Yanks did score were put across in the ninth, after Alexander had left the game – with a mixed smorgasbord of garbage and mustard.

Alexander is a control pitcher who puts the ball in play. He commands a varied repertoire of junk, which he throws mostly for strikes around the corners of the plate. On the mound he looks like a gunslinger – lanky, a little stoop-backed, thin beard on a gaunt face,* quiet narrow eyes sizing up the batter. He is only thirty-four but has been around the majors thirteen years – a rookie summer with the Dodgers in 1971; a key player in the trade that sent Frank Robinson from Baltimore to L.A. that winter; four-plus seasons with the Orioles; six-plus seasons drifting to the Yanks to Texas to Atlanta to San Francisco and back to the Yanks; and, finally, 1983, when he was picked up by the Jays and nailed down a spot in the starting rotation. Among the 115 games he has won in his travels is at least one against each of the majors' twenty-six clubs, and he is walking evidence that, in pitching, savvy matters. He is not among the game's most overpowering or gifted hurlers, but he is one of the smartest.

In the third game of the set the Yanks administered Toronto the worst shellacking they had endured since last season, 15-2. Again it was Clancy, who has not been sharp lately, who took the rap for the Jays. Nor was Bryan Clark sharp; if he did, as advertised, turn it around in Syracuse, he did not necessarily bring it to Toronto. In three and two-thirds innings' work he surrendered five hits, five walks, and four runs and threw two wild pitches – not a perfor-

---

* Shortly after this was written, Alexander shaved. He still, however, would look at home in the opening scenes of *High Noon*.

mance that will give Cox a whole lot of confidence about trotting him out at tricky moments in Detroit this week.

And so the outcome of the Yankee series hung on the second game, an absurd and sprawling affair – four hours, ten innings, forty ballplayers, and twenty-three l.o.b.'s – in which the Jays had a two-run lead (4-2), blew it, a three-run lead (7-4), blew it, and a one-run lead (8-7) entering the ninth, which they also blew. They eventually salvaged matters in the tenth on the strength of no (0) hits. Dave Collins was hit by a pitch. Alfredo Griffin reached first on a fielder's choice, forcing Collins, then moved to second on a error. Two Yank pitchers walked successive Jays to load the bases. And Ernie Whitt knocked a sac. fly. Not an artwork. But, for all that, it was the Jays' nineteenth consecutive win in a one-run game, a stat which has started to add up. They have not dropped a one-run match since the first week of the season when they lost three. And although one may rag the Jays about late-inning capers with loaded revolvers, the fact remains they have in these close games time and again hung on, pulled them out, found a way to win, which is the main reason why they are playing to date the second-best ball in the majors.

Standings, A.L. East, June 4

	W	L	PCT.	GB
Detroit	38	11	.776	—
Toronto	34	16	.680	4½
Baltimore	30	22	.577	9½
Boston	24	26	.480	14½
Milwaukee	22	27	.449	16
New York	21	29	.420	17½
Cleveland	17	31	.354	20½

SEVEN

Dribs and Drabs:
Snapshots and
Cautionary Tales

Baseball gives up its secrets in dribs and drabs.
— Tom Boswell

Any time you think you have the game conquered, the
game will turn around and punch you right in the nose.
— Mike Schmidt

June 14

Composing an all-star team of Detroit Tigers is a trek through baseball history. There is a dilemma in the outfield, only three spots available but four claimants, Sam Crawford (1903-17), Ty Cobb (1905-26), Harry Heilmann (1914-29), and Al Kaline (1953-74), and so one may be forced to sit on the bench, either the game's leading triples hitter, Crawford, or a four-time batting champ and lifetime .342 hitter, Heilmann. Either could, of course, play first, but Hank Greenberg (1930-46) is already there. Hence, Norm Cash (1960-74) is on the bench, too, although Cash and Rudy York (1934-45) offer the hot-stove manager a devastating left/right pinch-hitting combo. Around the horn, Charlie Gehringer (1924-42), a fine fielder and murderous doubles hitter, is at second; George Kell (1946-52) is at third. The choice at shortstop is between Donie Bush (1908-21), the better glove man, or Harvey Kuenn (1952-60), a .300 singles hitter.* Behind the plate is Bill Freehan (1961-76) who, in more than fifteen hundred games caught for the Tabs, a vital stat itself, compiled baseball's highest fielding average for a catcher ever.

Hurling from the left side are Hal Newhouser (1939-53), the only pitcher to have ever won consecutive league m.v.p. awards (1944 and 1945), and Mickey Lolich (1963-75). For righties, besides Tommy Bridges (1930-46), there are Hooks Dauss (1912-26), Schoolboy Rowe (1933-42), Dizzy Trout (1939-52), and Virgil Trucks (1941-52). Working in the bullpen is southpaw John Hiller (1965-78), hometown: Toronto, Ont.

There may be argument about some of these choices, but inciting argument is a main reason for making up such a list in the first place. And whatever argument there is will

---

* In the wake of the 1984 season, one is inclined to give Alan Trammell the nod over Kuenn here.

not blunt the proposition that, decade by decade, the Tigers have included some of baseball's fine players.

Tiger All-Stars (Career Stats)

		H	R	RBI	HR	BA	SA
1B	Hank Greenberg	1628	1051	1276	331	.313	.605
2B	Charlie Gehringer	2839	1774	1427	184	.320	.480
3B	George Kell	2054	881	870	78	.306	.414
SS*	Donie Bush	1804	1280	436	9	.250	.300
	Harvey Kuenn	2092	951	671	87	.303	.408
OF	Ty Cobb	4191	2244	1959	118	.367	.513
	Sam Crawford	2964	1393	1525	97	.309	.452
	Harry Heilmann	2660	1291	1551	183	.342	.520
	Al Kaline	3007	1622	1583	399	.297	.480
C	Bill Freehan	1591	706	758	200	.262	.412
PH	Norm Cash	1820	1046	1103	377	.271	.488
	Rudy York	1621	876	1152	277	.275	.483

		W	L	PCT.	ERA	SV
RHP	Tommy Bridges	194	138	.584	3.57	10
	Hooks Dauss	221	183	.547	3.32	39
	Schoolboy Rowe	158	101	.610	3.87	12
	Dizzy Trout	170	161	.514	3.23	35
	Virgil Trucks	177	135	.567	3.39	30
LHP	Hal Newhouser	207	150	.580	3.06	26
	Mickey Lolich	217	189	.534	3.42	11
	John Hiller	82	69	.543	2.63	116

		H	R	RBI	HR	BA	SA
*SS	Alan Trammell	985	516	372	56	.285	.397

As a franchise, however, their record has been curious. The Tigers have played the American League's second-best ball, but have won only eight pennants and since 1909 only five:

American League Standings, 1901–1983
(Original Franchises)

	W	L	T	PCT.	GB
New York[a]	7237	5494	90	.568	—
Detroit	6613	6162	93	.518	646
Cleveland	6552	6200	89	.514	695½
Boston	6484	6261	83	.509	760
Chicago	6419	6318	98	.504	821
Baltimore[b]	6072	6665	105	.477	1168
Minnesota[c]	6072	6706	107	.476	1188½
Oakland[d]	6012	6704	87	.473	1217½

a – Baltimore, 1901–02.
b – Milwaukee, 1901; St. Louis, 1902–53.
c – Washington, 1901–60.
d – Philadelphia, 1901–54; Kansas City, 1955–67.

This Tiger paradox between games won and flags won is explained partly by the dominance of the league by the Yankees, but only partly: Detroit finished second to New York in only five of the Yanks' thirty-three pennant-winning seasons. More to the point, the Tigers have been, year after year, a solid middle of the pack club, rarely near the bottom – they have trailed the A.L. only twice, in 1952 and 1975 – but also not so often at the top. This sort of franchise pattern suggests an interesting choice that might be offered Tiger fans: have they preferred the sturdy but staid respectability their club has habitually provided? (Bill James has described Tiger history pithily: "When patience was needed, they have always had patience. When a sense of urgency was needed, they have always had patience instead.") Or would they have preferred the ball played by the Philly-K.C.-Oakland A's, on three different occasions baseball's superpower but, on balance, the A.L.'s losingest club.

This is, of course, not a real choice. Fans become entwined with the character of clubs whose fortunes they follow – hence, the fatalism of Red Sox rooters, combativeness of the White Sox crowd, cockiness of Yankee boosters, and, at the moment, uncertain hopefulness of Blue Jay fans (still more familiar with ways things can go wrong than ways they can go right, but they are learning). In spite of decades of near things, busted optimism and wait-till-next-year's, Tiger fans would not trade their club. There has rarely been utter defeat. From Sam Crawford to Lance Parrish, there have always been good ballplayers to root for. And the Tigers have, at least once each generation, been the A.L.'s bona fide champs. What they are saying in Tigertown at the moment is that maybe 1984 is the next next year.

The collision of the Jays and Detroits provided seven games of riveting baseball full of lessons about how the game is played, won, and lost. In the end the Jays prevailed, four to three, convincingly; by the final two matches, both runaways, the Tigers were dead in the water. But during a three-day interruption of the set (after four games in Detroit, split two-two, before three final games in T.O.), the Jays journeyed to New York and were annihilated by the Yanks, and the Tigers visited Baltimore, where they cleaned the Orioles' clock, abruptly terminating, for the moment, rumours of the Orioles' invincibility. The outcome is that the A.L. East standings are roughly where they were two weeks ago.

Some dribs and drabs, then, about how baseball is lost, how, in Mike Schmidt's phrasing, it punches its practitioners in the nose:

•   *He makes pretty good ice cream, too.* Tiger set, game one, inning seven. The Jays lead 3-0 on homers by Willie Upshaw and George Bell. Dave Stieb has held the Ti's to three lonely hits and works the frame's first batter for a groundout. He then plonks centrefielder Chet Lemon. (Stat.

note: Stieb led A.L. pitchers last year in hit batsmen; Lemon led A.L. batters in getting hit.) First baseman Dave Bergman whacks a bad pitch, a slow curve, for a single, and up to the plate steps third sacker Howard Johnson, whom Stieb works to a two-two count. Johnson now guesses fastball (just a hunch, he says later), and Stieb pitches fastball, a cookie down the middle. Johnson is a little in front of it and whomps it down the rightfield line, hooking, hooking, hooking fou – *clonk*. The ball ricochets high off the foul pole mesh, and the game is tied.

• *Mother Jackson said there would be days like this.* Same game, inning ten, score still knotted 3-3. Jimmy Key is pitching, Lance Parrish has led off with a single, and d.h. Darrell Evans has sacrificed him to second. Bunting the d.h. is conservative ball, but the game has been a taut one, and Detroit skipper Sparky Anderson wants only the single run he needs to win it.

Bobby Cox replaces Key with Roy Lee Jackson to pitch to righty outfielder Rusty Kuntz, and Jackson logs the second out, retiring Kuntz on an easy comebacker. Jackson pitches around the dangerous Lemon – careful ball – creating a force at all three bases. The next batter is Bergman, whom the Tigers acquired just prior to the season mainly for his defensive skills; a lifetime .250 hitter, he is an excellent infielder. One remembers it was Bergman who made two sterling late-inning plays to protect Jack Morris's no-hitter back in April, and pieces of the Tiger puzzle are beginning to fall into place. They have a lot of ballplayers of the kind managers call "role-players": they are very good at specific jobs and do a lot of platooning. Weaver's Orioles were partly built around players like these. The Jays have a few who fit the mold. The Tigers appear to have several.

After three pitches Jackson is ahead of Bergman one-and-two. Bergman fouls a couple off. Jackson, whose work is meditative at the best of times, is rushing nothing, and there is a lot of cat and mouse as Jackson and Bergman alternately step off the rubber, step out of the box. Jackson tosses a fastball away which does not quite nick the plate and freezes Bergman. "I should have been swinging on that pitch," he will say later. The ump pauses and calls it a ball. Bergman now fouls off one . . . two . . . three . . . four . . . five successive pitches, then takes a ball, just outside. Full count.

Bergman's at-bat has lasted nearly eight minutes. Jackson's thirteenth pitch is a good hard slider, low, a pitcher's pitch. Bergman hesitates, then cranks it into the upper rightfield bleachers, his first homer of the season, his sixteenth in eight years in the majors. The game is suddenly over. (It has been, in spite of the Jays' loss, a memorable corker, crackling with a quality of play and tension that do not usually occur until autumn. The Jays and their fans have waited more than seven years for this, for ball games which matter.)

• *Along came Jones.* Tiger set, game four, inning six. Jim Clancy is working against Jack Morris. They have both had their stuff through five, and the score is tied 1-1. Lance Parrish leads off the frame with a wrong-field single, a nice bit of hitting. Clancy, who seems momentarily thrown off his game, overthrows to Darrell Evans – he is missing high – and walks him. Next up is John Grubb, a lefthanded hitter with some power, but Sparky Anderson ignores his power and puts on the bunt, again playing one-run ball. Grubb bunts foul, bunts foul again, and now must swing away; he pops to left. The next batter is Rupert Jones.

Jones, a Tiger less than forty-eight hours – two days ago he was playing minor league ball in Evansville – has been around. He was the Seattle Mariners' first pick in the 1977 Mariner/Jay expansion draft. (The Jays' was Bob Bailor.) His game never caught fire in Seattle, and a few years later he was traded to the Yankees, where he lasted a year before a trade to San Diego. His first season with the Padres was undistinguished, but in spring of 1982 Jones suddenly became the ballplayer everyone had hoped he might, hitting

.300 with power, driving in bunches of runs, carrying his club. He earned a berth on the N.L. All-Star club.

The year's second half was another story. Jones got stuck in a slump, was labelled a "problem" player, and ended up in manager Dick Williams' doghouse. The Padres did keep Jones through 1983 – he had a lacklustre year – at which point he became a free agent. No one was interested. Finally, early this spring, the Pirates, hungry for outfielders, offered him a tryout; no promises, just a look. They did not like what they saw and cut him, and it seemed he was out of the game. A month later the Tigers signed him to a minor league contract; again no promises. He tore up the bushies at about an r.b.i. a game, and now, with Anderson thinking he needs a little more punch, Jones is back in the majors. He is in centre today because Chet Lemon's back is bothering him and because the Jays are pitching a righty.

As Jones steps toward the plate, Bobby Cox trots to the mound to settle down Clancy. A d.p. will get the Jays out of the inning, and Cox did not like the look of Clancy's high stuff to Evans. Cox returns to the dugout, Jones steps in, and Clancy pitches – a fastball, again high. One-and-oh. Clancy now throws a slider that doesn't, does nothing, just hangs there, and Jones rides it to the upper rightfield deck, the gamebreaker.

- *You can't always get what you want, and sometimes you can't get what you need either.* Yankee set, game one. The match is tied at three in the bottom of the eleventh. The pitching and defence have been effective, the hitting has not, and each club has done its scoring a run at a time. Jim Acker, in relief of Jim Gott, has quickly retired two dangerous New York bats, Don Mattingly and Don Baylor. Next up is Dave Winfield. Cox has Garth Iorg, at third, guarding the foul line, and Winfield cracks a hard grounder deep in the shortstop hole that Iorg, positioned normally, might have had. Alfredo Griffin, somehow, gets his glove on the ball but cannot make the good peg. His throw pulls Willie Upshaw off the bag, and Winfield is aboard. The batter is now

Steve Kemp, who has lately been killing the Jays – twelve for seventeen in three-plus games since June 1. Acker has barely begun to work to Kemp when Winfield steals second. But Winfield is not the problem, Kemp is the problem – the inning's third out. And Acker gets him; Kemp knocks a routine grounder to Damaso Garcia. The ball suddenly hops like a frog over Garcia's head and into rightfield, and Winfield scores easily. An infield hit, a stolen base, a bad-hop single, and a game in the loss column. The Jays' string of wins in one-run games ends at nineteen.

- *Did anyone get the number of that truck?* Yankee set, game two. Dave Stieb pitches a fine game, fettering the Yanks to two slim runs. But Ron Guidry holds the Jays to but a single unearned run. (The Cajun, on his game, is maybe the classiest pitcher in the league.) Another one-run game is lost.

- *Buy that man a pair of glasses.* Yankee set, game three, inning eight. The Jays are down 5-3. Rance Mulliniks raps a one-out single, Ernie Whitt singles, and Willie Aikens comes to the plate, the go-ahead run. Yank manager Yogi Berra goes to the pen for lefty Bob Shirley, and Shirley, who cannot find the strike zone, walks Aikens on four high balls. Damaso Garcia comes up, and Shirley offers more high stuff, two-and-oh, then a curve that nicks the corner, two-and-one. Shirley's fourth pitch to Garcia is another high ball. His fifth is yet another high ball, or so it seems to nearly everyone who sees it. The ump, however, is of another view and pumps his fist. Say *what?* (Shirley himself later says with a smile that he was awfully lucky to get the pitch.) Garcia, badly exercised, remains at the plate, the bases stay loaded. Garcia lines Shirley's next pitch back to the box, and Shirley stabs it and pegs to first to double off the runner. Inning over. In the ninth the Jays die quietly.

- *Sam, you made the scores too short.* Yankee set, games one, two, three. Average ten hits an outing, and you will win some ball games, yes? Maybe, maybe not. The

Jays tallied thirty-one hits in New York. They also left thirty-one men on base, a lot of them in scoring position who got there with less than two out. They had nine more base runners who walked, a hit batsman, and a couple more who reached base on Yank errors. They scored seven meagre runs. Subtract the numbers against Guidry, and the picture is worse. In the other two games the Jays batted .303 and lost both – twenty-four l.o.b.'s. Bottom line: bad baseball.

Put another way, a bad-hop hit and an ump's gaffe make good stories, but they don't necessarily explain why a couple of games are lost. Had the Jays driven in more runs, neither Kemp's frog-ball nor Shirley's neck-high strike would have mattered, might not even have happened. The truism that bad breaks occur but over the course of the schedule are neutralized by good breaks is not relevant here. The Jays were not beaten in those games by bad breaks; they beat themselves. Their recent string of one-run wins was good ball but also lucky ball, hooked on the happy premise that bad breaks would not happen and good breaks would. It is nice when things work out this way, but it is not a principle to build a game plan on. Clubs who win at this game, win flags, the Series, win in spite of breaks, win when breaks are running against them. They don't *need* good breaks. The Jays are capable of streaks of fine ball, but whether they are seasoned enough to take it to the wire in the A.L. East is a question still not answered.

- *I got it! I got it! I – oops. (Outfield follies 1 and 2.)*

(1) Yankee set, game three, inning two. The Jays lead 1-0. The Yanks are at bat with two out and one on. Toby Hurrah lofts a fly to right-centre on which Lloyd Moseby and Jesse Barfield converge. Abruptly, both stop – whose ball? your ball? my ball? The ball drops, no third out, and the base runner scores. Tie game.

(2) One of the toughest plays in the outfield is the low hard line drive hit straight at you; because of the ball's angle, there is no geometry to work with in judging trajec-

tory. Tiger set, game five, inning one. Alan Trammell lines one at Moseby who takes a couple of steps back and realizes too late the ball will drop in front of him. Instead of letting it fall for a single, he tries to make up for his initial misjudgement with a shoestring catch he does not make. The ball hops through to deep centre, and Trammell ends up on third. He scores a moment later on an s.f.. Detroit 1, Jays 0. Same game, inning two. The Tigers have scored a second run, John Grubb is on second, and Rupert Jones is batting. Jones lines one at George Bell who takes a couple of steps back and realizes too late, etc. – see above. Jones ends up on second, Grubb scores, Ti's 3, Jays 0. The final score is 5-4 Detroit, another one-run match lost, another drib-and-drab of evidence that little things matter in this game.*

So much for cautionary tales. The Detroit set also offered snapshots of how baseball is won:

• *A running Blue Jay gathers no moss.* Tiger set, game one (which the Jays ultimately lost), inning six. The Jays lead 1-0 on Willie Upshaw's homer in the second, and Upshaw is now at first on a one-out single. Willie Aikens, not a fast runner, raps a grounder to second, a sure double-play ball, except Upshaw was running on the pitch; the Tigers' only play is at first. The Jays' inning stays alive, and the next batter, George Bell, rams a home run to deep left-centre, Jays 3, Ti's 0. Staying out of the d.p. is something the Jays have been doing effectively this season – Bobby Cox habitually sends the runner on first on two-one and three-one counts – and they have thus far grounded into fewer d.p.'s than any club in the league.

* The Jay outfielders took their lessons to heart. There were few similar gaffes during the rest of the season.

100

- *Tigerburgers.* Tiger set, game two, inning four. It is not clear yet that the Jays can play ball with the Tigers. In game one Detroit beat the Jays' best, Dave Stieb and Roy Jackson, and after three frames in game two the Jays are down 2-1 and shaky. Aside from a homer by Moseby, they have yet to hit a ball out of the infield, and Doyle Alexander is not sharp. He is missing high, falling behind, and last inning walked two batters in a row. The Jays and their fans need a lift, a change of karma, a tangible sign they are seriously in this thing, before this game starts to slip out of control.

Moseby, leading off, hammers a triple to deep, deep centre and scores a moment later on an infield groundout by Willie Upshaw. Tie game and a gold star for Moseby (seven bases in two at-bats) but no real shift of mood yet, just a faint ray of light. Willie Aikens rams a homer – Jays 3, Tigers 2 – and George Bell and Rance Mulliniks chase Detroit starter Glenn Abbott from the game with a pair of singles. The light is getting stronger; Jay fans are starting, albeit skittishly, to smile a little. Abbott is replaced by Doug Bair, who works Ernie Whitt to a one-two count at which point Whitt deposits a Bair fastball in the upper rightfield deck. Jays 6, Tigers 2; the smiles are turning to grins. Alfredo Griffin slams another Bair offering into the upper rightfield deck. Jays 7, Tigers 2; the Jays will go on to win 8-4.

There are moments in baseball when a player rises to an occasion and alters it. A random memory – 1975, the World Series, Game Six, among the best ball games ever played. In the bottom of the eighth, with two out, two on, and Cincinatti ahead 6-3, Boston skipper Darrell Johnson sent part-time outfielder Bernie Carbo to bat for the Bosock pitcher. Red reliever Rawly Eastwick's first pitch was a fastball on the hands at which Carbo hacked. Strike one. Eastwick then put a fastball out over the plate, a tad high, and Carbo swung again and connected. The ball came to rest in Fenway Park's centrefield bleachers, and the game was tied.

Carlton Fisk's home run down the leftfield foul line four innings later became the enduring image of the game, but it was Carbo's earlier homer which made Fisk's heroics possible.

On other occasions, a whole team snatches the moment. The Chicago Cubs were cruising with an 8-0 lead over Connie Mack's A's in the seventh inning of the fourth game of the 1929 World Series. A Cub win in the game would lock the Series at two-all. In that seventh inning the A's rallied for ten hits and ten runs and broke the Cubs' heart.

Here in the Detroit set it is the full Jay offence that announces its presence and alters the occasion. The Jays know now Detroit can be had, and in game three, the following evening, eight Jay batters scatter thirteen hits – including an upperdeck homer by Upshaw and an inside-the-park homer by George Bell – good for six runs. Luis Leal and Dennis Lamp get the pitching job done. Leal's work is not pretty – he gives up eight hits and five walks – but he holds the Ti's down. Lamp closes the final two frames on six ground-ball outs. With the win the Jays pull to within three and a half games of the Tigers, the closest they have been since mid-April. Maybe there will be a pennant race after all.

• *Davey Sparkplug.* Five days later, after five losses to Detroit and New York, the Jays are eight games back and looking tight and punchy. Tonight's pitching matchup, for the sixth game of the Detroit set, is not encouraging: Jim Clancy, who has been rocked in his last three starts, will face Jack Morris, the Tigers' ace. By the time the game is two batters old, matters look dark. Lou Whitaker has led off with a first-pitch double, and Clancy has then quickly walked Alan Trammell. But Clancy, working like a man sitting on a pile of TNT, manages to snuff the threat. His slider, the pitch that has lately failed him, has its pop, and he suckers Kirk Gibson into a Garcia-to-Griffin-to-Upshaw d.p. He then retires Lance Parrish, also on a groundout, and Whitaker dies on third.

Now it is the Jays' ups. Damaso Garcia doubles, and Dave Collins comes to bat. In the Jays' loss last night Collins whacked a three-run homer that nearly kept them in it. Before tonight's game he called a club meeting, players only, to clear the air after the five-day losing spree. His at-bat now, though the match is only half a frame gone, will be the game's turning point – a turning point, too, in the Jay/Tiger series. Collins lashes a triple to drive home Garcia. Two innings later he scores the game's second run, fashions it from speed. He beats out an infield grounder, steals second, and scores on a shallow base hit.

Like Rupert Jones, Collins was a Seattle Mariner expansion draftee, taken from the Angels, with whom he logged two major league seasons. He played one undistinguished year in Seattle and was traded to Cincinnati where, for another year, he mostly rode the bench. The Reds' outfield from their championship mid-seventies clubs, George Foster, Ken Griffey, and Cesar Geronimo, was still intact – little room for a newcomer. But the following year, 1979, Foster and Griffey both spent time on the injury list, and Collins logged nearly 400 at-bats in more than 120 games. He hit .318, mostly singles; he has no power. In 1980, playing full time, he again hit .300 and stole seventy-nine bases.

The next year his numbers fell off, but it was those earlier stats George Steinbrenner had in mind when he signed Collins to a fat free-agent contract in 1982. Steinbrenner was creating a new-look jackrabbit Yankee club, a concept that lasted approximately a month and a half. New York management seemed to have no idea, once they had him, what to do with Collins. He played some outfield, first base, d.h., never sure from one day to the next where or whether he would be playing. He became an unproductive ballplayer, which ran maddeningly against his grain; he became a badly disgruntled ballplayer. That winter he was swapped to Toronto.

Bothered by a recurrent leg injury, he had a rotten first half in 1983. And like most players who arrive in a new town, he did not really look like a Blue Jay – more like that guy who used to be a Red and, now in a Blue Jay uniform, seemed a little out of place. But after the All-Star break he was back to his old ways, hitting .300, swiping bases, igniting rallies with speed and beginning to look more at home. This year he has mostly platooned with Jesse Barfield – Collins against righties, Barfield against lefties – and has been a key factor in the Jays' attack, partly because of his skills, partly as a sparkplug who gets things happening. When the Jays are breaking a game open, Collins is usually somewhere in the middle of it.

The Tigers, it seems, never had a chance in this game. The Jays knock out Jack Morris in a six-run fourth, and later Ernie Whitt tags his second three-run homer of the week. (Whitt, whose hometown is Detroit, loves to hit against the Tigers. He nailed six of his seventeen homers last year against Tiger pitching.) The final score is Jays 12, Detroit 3, and the series is tied at three games each.

• *Quiet ballplayer, noisy bat.* Willie Upshaw does not look a lot like a ballplayer – maybe more like a young lawyer or business exec – and does not have a lot to say. Quiet type. Take him out of the Jay lineup, and they would be a different team.

Tiger set, game seven, inning seven. The Tigers have no runs – they cannot solve Dave Stieb – and the Jays have five. With two out Dave Collins and Lloyd Moseby rap singles, and Upshaw slams a double that drives home both runners. (In the seven Detroit games he has now driven in nine runs.) Any chance the Tigers had of playing catch-up is gone.

Upshaw probably ought to be a Yankee today. Before Don Mattingly, first base was a Yankee problem. Since the trade of Chris Chambliss, they had tried ten or more players at the position: Jim Spencer, Bob Watson, John Mayberry, Dave Revering, Ken Griffey, Dave Collins, etc., none to very good effect. Had they had Willie Upshaw in the minors, he might have stepped in and claimed the job as Mattingly has, but Upshaw was long gone to Toronto, snatched in the 1977 minor league draft. There was special irony in the fact that the Yanks tried Mayberry at first after he had lost his job in Toronto to the Yanks' own former prospect, Upshaw.

In any case, bringing along minor-leaguers has not, in recent years, been the Yankee way; it is a process which needs patience, and George Steinbrenner has no patience. Today, the Yankees are mostly an assortment of high-priced, high-powered spare parts, while the teams that dominate the division – Detroit, Toronto, Baltimore – are made up mainly of farm system products and of role-player ballplayers acquired in trades. (The Tigers – another piece of the puzzle – have only a single free agent on their roster, d.h.-infielder Evans, signed, as the Jays signed Dennis Lamp, to plug a gap that the farm and trades left unfilled.) While one respects many of the Yankee ballplayers, there is something hollow about the club as a whole, maybe because one of the most involving dimensions of rooting for a club – watching youngsters come along, master their game, become ballplayers – is mostly absent. Fans in Detroit and Toronto have been watching these Tigers and Jays, now tearing up the league, mature from sprouts, grow into winning.* (There is also a special pleasure in watching a journeyman no-name ballplayer acquired in a trade, a Dave Bergman or Rance Mulliniks, find his niche with your club; but that is another story.) One of the sprouts they have watched grow in Toronto is Upshaw.

---

* Shortly after this was written the Yanks began to give a clutch of youngsters a whole lot more playing time. Simultaneously, they began winning a whole lot more ball games and became, under Yogi Berra's tutelage, a more interesting club.

	W	L	PCT.	GB
Detroit	44	16	.733	—
Toronto	38	22	.633	6
Baltimore	35	27	.565	10
Boston	31	29	.517	13
New York	26	33	.441	17½
Milwaukee	25	34	.424	18½
Cleveland	22	35	.386	20½

EIGHT

In and out of a Mudhole

When the pressure builds up, it's like being in a bus in a mudhole. The harder you press the pedal, the farther you sink in the mud.
— Bob Watson

There are a hundred and fifty-four games in a season, and you can find a hundred and fifty-four reasons why your team should have won every one of them.
— Bill Klem

June 28

Again, there is good news and bad news.

The good news is Luis Leal. He has, to date, won eight, lost two, and compiled an e.r.a. of 2.79, and the Jays are thirteen and four in games Leal has started, four losses that were all avoidable.

Leal has not always been artful, but in none of his seventeen starts has he failed to keep the Jays in the game. He is yet to be badly rocked or come unstrung in late innings. In the two losses with which he was charged he pitched well but was undone by circumstance; one, for instance, was the 5-4 Detroit loss in which the Jay outfield did its impression of a sieve. In his other two starts which were lost, the Jays had a lead when he left the game. And on occasion he has been highly artful. Cases in point: twice in the last two weeks he has faced the Bosox, a club who can hit; they lead the majors in homers. Leal's record in the two outings: eighteen innings pitched for two complete games; six hits, two walks, and two runs allowed; and two wins. The kind of pitcher he is may vary. In one of the games against the Sox one of his main weapons was the strikeout; he K-ed nine. In the other he whiffed none, letting his fielders do the work, hence needed only eighty-one pitches to get the job done, a model of economy.

On the mound, Leal seems laconic. He is usually poker-faced, his wind-up and delivery loose and fluid. His repertoire includes a fastball, slider, curve, and change, none remarkable in itself, but effective when he mixes them well. Now and then he seems careless – he will, out of the blue, surrender an opponent a couple of walks almost, it appears, because he cannot quite keep in the game. But the appearance is deceiving. Leal's mind is on his work, and these lapses are more a consequence of excessive care than carelessness – an occasional tendency to worry his pitches, nibble too cautiously at the corners. Once he is in trouble and has to bear down, there is a slight shift in his style, a hint of fretfulness in his eyes, more snap in the liquid swivel of his hips and easy sweep of his arm. But at no time does he seem especially excited.

The contrast of Leal's manner and Dave Stieb's is marked. Stieb works quickly, intensely; he does not believe *anyone* should get on base against him. When he gets in trouble, the cockiness turns to anger, and he paces behind the rubber between pitches whacking the ball in his glove and muttering darkly to himself like a demented old ragpicker. When he has pitched out of a jam, and the inning is over, he sprints across the infield to the dugout like a demon is after him – this man is fired *up*. It is hard to imagine Leal sprinting anywhere if the choice of a stroll is available.

Partly because he does not evidence a lot of hard-nosed emotion, Leal has sometimes been labelled not aggressive enough. But good pitching does not necessarily require making a show of hostility. Bob Gibson, of course, did – visibly regarded each batter as an enemy to be obliterated. (Gibson's 1.12 e.r.a. in 1968 may be the most remarkable feat in modern pitching.) Catfish Hunter, on the other hand, often looked as though he had just wandered into the park from a turkey shoot and would rather be taking a nap.

Leal has thrown as well before – some outings here, outings there – but never so consistently as this season. There may be several reasons why he seems to have found his game. He is older now, twenty-seven, and more in command of his skills. He seems surer of them. He pitched at home in Venezuela less last winter than in past and has a fresher arm this year. He is throwing fewer home-run balls than was his habit in earlier seasons.*

The game in which Leal required only eighty-one pitches to dispatch the Red Sox was played in Fenway Park. John Updike wrote about Fenway, it "is a lyric little bandbox of

---

* Leal stayed tough through August, then seemed to tire and also had some bad luck. He did not win a game in September.

a ballpark. Everything is painted green and seems in curiously sharp focus, like the inside of an old-fashioned peeping-type Easter egg." Wrigley Field, Comiskey Park (Chicagoans are twice blessed), Tiger Stadium, even Yankee Stadium, though it has been renovated, evoke like emotions. Old parks have tradition; old clubs have it, too, though it is harder to sense if they have moved into one of the modern cookie-cutter ballparks or gone a couple of thousand miles across the continent.

In Fenway one looks out at leftfield where Jim Rice plays (Rice is, of course, a member of the all-time all-grain outfield, with Zach Wheat and Willie Mays) and sees the ghosts of Yaz and Ted Williams. Apart from Williams' war years and a couple of seasons when Yastrzemski played other positions, leftfield in Fenway has been patrolled by one of these three since 1940, and Rice's career is long from over. One may browse the encyclopedias for hours and not find another notch in the game's history lodged with as formidable a lineage of baseball talent. There have been notable two-player sequences. The Yanks, for example, had Bill Dickey and Yogi Berra behind the plate from 1929 until 1961 and Joe Dimaggio and Mickey Mantle in centrefield from 1936 until 1966. But successions of three remarkable ballplayers are much rarer. The nearest one may come to the Williams/Yastrzemski/Rice triad may have been at shortstop for the Chicago White Sox from 1931 until 1962 – Luke Appling, Chico Carresquel, and Luis Aparicio.

Tradition is something that expansion ballclubs do not have. A Toronto fan may remember Al Woods fondly, but it is not quite the same thing as remembering Roberto Clemente, much less trying to see in the mind's eye how Pie Traynor or Honus Wagner may have played (to name a few Pirates, a club deep in tradition). And so it is not inappropriate that expansion clubs should have to work so long and hard to gain respect. Among baseball's qualities is resistance of the fly-by-night.

The Red Sox are a curious club because one thought

one knew them well. But that was a few years ago, and now one discovers one does not know them very well at all. Carlton Fisk, Fred Lynn, Rick Burleson, and now even Yaz are gone – gone, except Yaz, a while ago. Yet so vivid a club were the seventies Sox that one still half expects to see them out there in their familiar uniforms at their familiar spots, having just one more go at it, a Homeric club undone by themselves and by vicissitudes of fate (*cf.* the collected works of Roger Angell). Rice and Dwight Evans do, at least, remain, and Rice has emerged as the A.L.'s most prodigious slugger of the eighties. Besides Rice and Evans, the current club is built around sluggers (Tony Armas, Mike Easler) and solid journeymen (Bill Buckner) acquired in trades and some talented younger players (Wade Boggs, Rick Gedman) brought up through the Sox system. The pitching staff is similarly composed. The club's personality is still emergent, and more changes are likely in the next year or two, further altering the chemistry. But, whoever they are, the Sox always seem to command the attention of serious ball fans, maybe partly because of that old park they play in. And the Sox have, this year, been pretty often playing interesting ball.

Fresh from their defeat of the mighty Tigers, the Jays hosted the Red Sox for three games in which their guests bowed pliantly. One of the matches, in particular, is worth a glance because it seems to tie up in a neat little package a lot of the ball the Jays have played this year.

They got highly serviceable starting pitching from Doyle Alexander, who, after nine innings, had surrendered only two runs. The Jays, however, though they had enjoyed base runners in droves – sixteen l.o.b.'s – had scored just one. They bided their time until there were two out and an oh-two count in the bottom of the ninth, a whisker from demise, to log the tying run. The batter was Moseby, who singled home Dave Collins, on second with a double. So the inning ended; the tenth was uneventful. In the eleventh the Jays permitted the Sox to score a go-ahead run on two cheap singles, an error by Jimmy Key, and a bases-loaded walk by Dennis Lamp. In the frame's bottom they again waited until they were down to their final strike before notching the tying and winning runs. Rance Mulliniks drove home Collins and Willie Upshaw. (*N.b.* Collins' role in these late-inning rallies.) When one thinks back on this year's Jays, a lot of the memories will be of games like these, squeaked out by the Cardiac Kids.

Matters do not always resolve themselves so benignly. (We are reaching the bad news.) In the Bosox' wake the Brewers rolled their barrel into town and twice beat the Jays at their own game, breaking tied matches with single runs in the ninth. In their final ups in both games the Jays folded – that old last-minute magic didn't happen. Chastened, the Jays adjourned to Boston for a four-game set with the Sox and won one, lost one, won one, and were ahead in the final match 3-0 with one out in the bottom of the ninth when disaster struck. Dave Stieb, who had thus far tossed a three-hitter, surrendered two singles, got the second out, then walked a batter to load the sacks and gave up a base-clearing game-tying double. In the tenth Dennis Lamp was touched for a single and a homer, and it was bye-bye ball game, another match nearly won but not quite. Next on the Jays' itinerary was Milwaukee; they may as well have come home.

The Brewers are another team one knew well just a short while ago: the Thumpers. In 1982, the year they won the A.L. flag, they rapped 216 homers, the most by a club in a season since 1964 when the Twins whacked 221. Gorman Thomas, Ben Oglivie, Cecil Cooper, Robin Yount – it was a club built on a bedrock of solid power. Last year Thomas was traded, and h.r. production was otherwise way down; the Brewers slipped to ninth in the league in round-trippers. This year, thus far, they are last – *last* – in the A.L. in homers.

COOL HAND KEY: The brightest spot among Jay pitchers during spring training was twenty-two-year-old Jimmy Key, who came to camp as a non-roster player, won three games and earned a spot in the bullpen. (*Toronto Blue Jays*)

OUCH! Lloyd Moseby hit his head against Robin Yount's knee sliding into second for a stolen base in an exhibition game against the Brewers in Vancouver April 1. Yount (l.) and second baseman Jim Gantner look down as Moseby momentarily rests his head on his arms. (*Canapress Photo Service*)

HOME AGAIN: The Jays opened the season with a six-and-four road trip, then returned home to Toronto for a three-game sweep of their old nemesis, the Baltimore Orioles. Here, Willie Upshaw slides safely into second as Cal Ripken is late with a tag. (*Canapress Photo Service*)

THE IRON MAN: Alfredo Griffin turns a d.p. across Lenn Sakata in the Jays' 2-1 win against Baltimore April 19. (*Canapress Photo Service*)

A JAY SINCE DAY ONE: Garth Iorg, one of the Jays' three remaining expansion draftees, was the star of the April 19 game, batting four-for-four, driving in both Toronto runs, and turning a couple of fine fielding plays. (*Toronto Blue Jays*)

DOWNTOWN: Lloyd Moseby whacked his first major league grand slam home run against California in Toronto April 20, and Willie Upshaw greeted him as he crossed the plate. The clout gave the Jays a 4-3 lead in the game, but in the end it didn't help. The Jay lost the match, and the Angels swept the series 3-0. (*Canapress Photo Service*)

CRUNCH: The Jays won a 2-1 thriller in Chicago May 30 as Dave Stieb notched his seventh victory of the young season. In the top of the seventh Ernie Whitt wiped out White Sox second baseman Julio Cruz to break up a double play. (*Canapress Photo Service*)

(above) STAR MATERIAL: The Jays won their home-and-away June series against the mighty Tigers four games to three. Among the stars of the sets was George Bell, here sliding safely into second for a stolen base as the ball gets by shortstop Alan Trammell. Bell was, for the season, among the brightest new young stars in the American League, playing exuberant and chancy ball and constantly beating the odds. (*Canapress Photo Service*)

(left) GOTCHA: Red Sox base-runner Rick Miller is out at first, tagged by Willie Upshaw in a game in Toronto June 15. Making the call is umpire Dave Phillips. The Jays won the game 4-3. (*Canapress Photo Service*)

SAFE: Red Sox third baseman Ed Jurak goes high for the throw and cannot make the tag as Damaso Garcia steals third in a game against Boston June 16. The Jays won 5-3 and notched a 3-0 sweep of the series. (*Canapress Photo Service*)

HITTING THE DIRT: Cliff Johnson is hit by a pitch by Red Sox hurler Bruce Hurst and goes down in the June 16 game. For the season, the Jays led the league in hit batsmen. *(Canapress Photo Service)*

SLUGGER: Jesse Barfield saw action in six games of the Jays' midseason homestand and batted .454 and slugged 1.182 in the matches, collecting a double, a triple, five homers and nine r.b.i.'s. (*Toronto Blue Jays*)

SPEEDSTER: Dave Collins beats the throw from home and takes out Angel shortstop Rob Picciolo in a game against the Angels July 4. For the season, Collins stole sixty bases, a new Jay club high. (*Canapress Photo Service*)

GOOSE GOTT: After the bullpen's difficult road trip in July, Bobby Cox posted fifth starter Jim Gott to the stopper's job. The results were mixed: Gott won some but also lost some. (*Toronto Blue Jays*)

RHUBARB: Bobby Cox steps between Dave Collins and umpire Mike Reilly in a game in Chicago August 20. Reilly had called Collins out on a play at first. Later in the game Collins hit a two-run triple, and the Jays won the match 7-4. (*Canapress Photo Service*)

THE KID:
Tony Fernandez, the Jays' young phenom shortstop, flips a peg to first to complete a double play against Cleveland on August 21. Dave Stieb pitched a complete game in the match, but the Jays lost it 3-1. (*Canapress Photo Service*)

BACKSTOP: Twin Kirby Puckett hands Buck Martinez a foul ball in a game in Toronto September 2, the Jays' final match of the year against West Division clubs. The Jays closed with their best record yet against the West, 52-32. (*Canapress Photo Service*)

CRAFTSMAN: The Jays' batting leader for the season was platoon thirdsacker Rance Mulliniks, who hit .324 in 343 at-bats. (*Toronto Blue Jays*)

DOLDRUMS: Willie Aikens knocked 23 homers and drove in 72 runs in 400 a.b.'s with the Royals in 1983. But after his difficult winter and late start, he was unable to produce as effectively for the Jays. (*Toronto Blue Jays*)

THE ROTATION, #1: The heart of the Jays was the club's front four starters, who were 61-35 for the season. The staff's ace, Dave Stieb, lost the A.L. e.r.a. title by a fraction, was the league's All-Star starter for the second year running and collected 16 Jay wins. (*Toronto Blue Jays*)

THE ROTATION, #2: In the fourteenth year of a career in which he has pitched for seven major league clubs, Doyle Alexander had his best year yet in 1984, with 17 wins and a 3.13 e.r.a. He is one of the smartest pitchers in the game. (*Toronto Blue Jays*)

THE ROTATION, #3: Through mid-August, Luis Leal was among the strongest pitchers in the league. The highlight of his season was a matched set of complete-game wins against Boston in June. (*Toronto Blue Jays*)

THE ROTATION, #4: Jim Clancy rode out a difficult slump at mid-season and finished the year with sub-par 13-15 record. But he also won some crucial games and was, over the summer, a workhorse, not missing a scheduled start. (*Toronto Blue Jays*)

THE END: The Jays' fragile pennant hopes died in Toronto September 7, 8 and 9, when the Tigers shattered the Jays' bullpen and swept a three-game set. In the fourth frame of the final match Ruppert Jones was out on a force at second. Damaso Garcia makes the play, and Tony Fernandez looks on. For the rest of September the Jays devoted their energies to hanging on to second place. (*Canapress Photo Service*)

(This astonishing decline in power is only part of the reason for the Brewers' tumble in the standings. They have also been plagued by an awful spate of injuries, especially to their pitchers.) But the Brewers can still hurt you. They strike out less than most clubs and have one of the best hit-and-run games in the league, and they have some veteran hitters – Cooper, Yount, Oglivie, Ted Simmons – who, if lately erratic, are always dangerous. Also, the Brewers appear to have the Jays' number this year.

The Jays played and lost four games in Milwaukee, yielding an oh-and-six record against the Brewers so far this season, six losses in the space of nine days. At least none of the County Stadium matches was kicked away in the final inning. The Brewers did the bulk of their scoring early on, blowing the Jays out in their first turn through the batting order.

Portrait of an abominable first inning: Luis Leal, sharp as usual, works the first two Brewer batters for harmless-seeming grounders. Both, however, slip just past Damaso Garcia's glove, one to his left, one to his right – the ball seems to have a mind of its own – for seeing-eye singles. A sac. fly drives a run home. Then, amid much confusion at second base involving Alfredo Griffin, Garcia, a base runner, and an ump (the ump seems to call the runner out with his right hand and safe with his left), then alters this to safe with his right hand and out with his left, the Jays are unable to log a force play; Griffin is charged, not quite fairly, with an error. The fifth Brewer batsman bloops a dying quail to right that drops just in front of a frantically onrushing George Bell, and the sixth nearly does the same to left, except Griffin makes an implausible play, snaring the ball about ten feet in the air. Now there is a grounder to Upshaw, easy out, but Upshaw boots it. The eighth Brewer finally gets the inning's first clean hit and drives in two runs. It might have been only one, but Buck Martinez takes the peg shaded slightly back in foul territory instead of blocking the plate and cannot make a tag on the second runner.* The next batter at last makes the third out, but four runs have scored, and the Jays are in a hole from which they will not dig out. Lord, there are a lot of ways you can lose this game. Leal leaves the mound looking a little shell-shocked.

The most memorable moment of the Brewer set – another baseball chestnut to hoard – occurred in the ninth inning of a match in which the Jays were trying to overtake a three-run Brewer lead. Garth Iorg pinch-hit a one-out single, bringing up George Bell who has been terrorizing A.L. hurling this season (b.a., an ugly .321). Milwaukee manager Rene Lachemann decided it was time for his stopper, Rollie Fingers, who has recovered in apparently good fettle from a career-threatening injury and whom we last met in Chapter One at 301 career saves. He is currently at 315 and counting. Abruptly, in the midst of an otherwise humdrum game, we were offered a mythic baseball confrontaton: redhot kid vs. savvy old pro. It was, maybe not unexpectedly, the savvy old pro who got the best of this one.

Word is out around the league that Bell nails the lowball, has more trouble with high ones, and Fingers' first offering – in his heyday he could pitch the whiskers off a cat – was a rib-high fastball on the inside edge of the plate which froze Bell like a statue. Fingers' second pitch looked a lot like the first, but he took a little something off it and put a little something on it, and it dematerialized and rematerialized a number of inches lower as it crossed the plate. Bell flailed like a man trying to swat a mosquito with a boat oar. Strike two. Fingers now broke off a hard singing curve at which Bell swung so viciously his helmet flew off. He missed. Strike three, easy as pie. The kid, looking perplexed (who

---

* Martinez's play here, if unaggressive, was maybe prudent. Ernie Whitt was on the disabled list at the time, and so injury to Martinez would have left the Jays without a backstop.

was that man?), retired to the dugout. Part way there he examined his bat (maybe there was a hole in it?). Fingers, one out closer to Cooperstown, waited on the mound, impassive, for his next victim. The Jays' nascent little rally presently expired.

By the time they departed Milwaukee, the Jays were no longer playing .600 ball and had dropped to ten games behind Detroit, only a couple ahead of Baltimore, flirting with third place. And though, in the games that had mattered most, they had bettered the Tigers, their record through the first four weeks of June, games played entirely against their A.L. East rivals, was a somewhat malodorous eleven and fifteen.

Jay fans are concerned by their club's slump into a mud-hole and have ideas about what may be wrong. One may catalogue nearly as many explanations as one knows Jay fans. There is likely a dabble of truth in many of them.

A lot of the Jays are young, and consistency does not always come easily to young ballplayers. And, as has already been noted, they are well down in the league in homers and, in partial consequence, are leaving a lot of runners on base. Too, the Jays are free-swingers and are way down in the league in bases on balls. They partly make up for this lack of walks with their hitting, but only partly. A stat: while the Tigers' b.a. is only a point higher than the Jays' (.281 to .280), their on-base average is sixteen points higher (.350 to .334), mainly an effect of free passes (270 vs. the Jays' 200). A corollary of the Jays' lowish rate of walks is a highish rate of strikeouts, slightly higher than the league average and a third again higher than the club with the fewest K's (the Yanks, who have 287 K's to the Jays' 371).The Jays have a habit of jumping on first pitches, not always wisely, and among Cito Caston's main jobs with the young Jay hitters has been teaching them patience – wait for your pitch and swing only at strikes – at which they still need to do some learning.*

For all that, a lot of what one can say about flaws in the Jays' offence is just so much grousing – statistically right but not necessarily right-headed. No one complains much about the Jays' free-swinging when the club is winning. And if the Jays have a weakness here, they maybe also have a strength: they lead the league in hits, doubles, and triples; nearly lead in several other offensive categories; and are almost impossible to shut out – only once in seventy-four games. They do need to score more runs. They are second in the league here, yet also trail the Tigers by sixty runs. They need more homers, more patience, more consistency. But offence has been only a part, maybe a small part, of what has gone wrong this month.

The trouble has not been defence either. The Jays are not a nine of Gold Gloves, and there has been the occasional bit of Three-Stooges-Play-Baseball that has cost a couple of games. But they are well up in the league defensively and have no conspicuous holes. And often their glovework has kept them *in* ball games, now and then saved a ball game.

Pitching is harder to figure. Jay fans are understandably jumpy about the bullpen. When something goes sour, they often look here first. And the pen's work has not been consistent this year. Roy Jackson has lately been steady, but Jimmy Key, strong at first, has tailed off, and Dennis Lamp and Jim Acker have up days and down days. All told, the pen has logged thirteen wins and sixteen saves but has also tallied eleven losses. More to the point, the Jays have lost to date a couple of dozen games in the final innings, and in most of those matches it was the pen that failed to stop the other side from scoring (they were not always the pitchers of record). One may explain away some of these lapses as functions of defensive miscues or the odd bad break or simply getting beat – you make the good pitch, but

* They did seem to learn. During the season's second half they lowered their strikeout ratio.

the other guy whams it. But the pen probably might have kept the club in at least half a dozen more ball games. Hence Pat Gillick has been beating the bushes for relief help and talked trade a couple of weeks ago with San Francisco – Stan Clarke for the Giants' veteran southpaw Gary Lavelle. But Clarke had to be taken off the swapping block when he developed tendinitis in his pitching shoulder.

Again, one is forced to compare the Jays' stats with the Tigers'. Detroit's frontline relievers, Willie Hernandez, Aurelio Lopez, and Doug Bair, have thus far logged twenty-five saves and a won/lost record of thirteen and one. (*N.b.*: comparisons of this kind are tricky. One cannot pan the Jays' pen for not being the Tigers' pen any more than one can pan a school of flounder for not being a flock of chickens. They are who they are and try to do their best at it.) But – a big *but* – only four of the Jays' fifteen losses during their June slide can be laid to rest with the bullpen.

Another five of the losses were the responsibility of the starting pitchers. (The remaining six losses fall into an "other" category: consequences of fielding balls-ups, lack of offence, or the whim of fate.) And here we find one current dilemma on the club: four of the starters' losses were charged to Jim Clancy; Clancy had a rotten June. He seems to be having trouble with some of his pitches, particularly his slider, and may also, in Bob Watson's phrasing, be pressing the pedal too hard. The month was not a complete wipeout. Clancy won two games, including a big one against Detroit, and he remains a workhorse; he has not missed a start since April. But he has not, lately, been a strong link in the rotation.

Slumps of this kind are something that happen to pitchers. Dave Stieb, for instance, was three-and-six last June and July, and Doyle Alexander was one-and-six last July and August. Clancy, meanwhile, was ten-and-four those months. It was only the legends – Christy Mathewson, Grover Alexander, Carl Hubbell, Warren Spahn – who rarely suffered hard times (even they had the odd dry spell), and the more baseball one sees, the more one appreciates the numbers beside their names. Alexander, for one, never had less than a .500 season except in his final year at age forty-three, yet he played on only three pennant-winning clubs. The betting line on Clancy is he will come around soon, win a batch of games, and right his season. Time will tell.

Finally, besides offence, defence, and pitching, there is the way the club is run – Bobby Cox's handling of pitchers and use of platoon strategies. The main notions about the former, depending on whom you talk to, are that he is leaving his starters in too long and yanking his starters too soon. Both ideas are rendered somewhat moot by the fact there is no apparent difference between his handling of the starters when the club is losing and when it is winning. Again, complaints tend to peter out when the Jays are winning. Cox does seem to put a lot of faith in young Jimmy Key, but Key is his only reliable southpaw; he has borne out Cox's faith, if irregularly, more often than not.

The main issue with the platoon system is in the outfield. With Bell playing daily, Collins hot, and Moseby a fixture, Jesse Barfield is warming a lot of bench. He has started only against lefties and has just 140-odd at-bats so far; and his glove and arm are not in rightfield those games. Like the Griffin/Fernandez dilemma, this outfield question is a real conundrum. The bottom line, however, is that Barfield is not playing nearly enough. The Jays badly need his power.

The picture that emerges is that the Jays did not have a lousy month for this or that or the other reason but for a batch of smaller and medium-sized reasons which, like rocks in a slide, added up to a stretch of .400 ball. Too, they ran up against a couple of hot clubs, the Yanks and Brewers, and against some pitchers who, with the season now well under way and word getting around about the Jays' long suits and blind spots, pitched them smarter; the Jays are pretty much a fastball-hitting club, preferably low fastballs. Again, age and seasoning matter; younger hitters have a harder time than more experienced hitters adjusting to pitchers who come after them.*

Baseball clubs do lose. Even good teams lose two games for every three they win, and they often do their losing in bunches. Losing – a momentary slump – is not in itself a problem; rather, it is the effect of losing that can be a problem – if a club gets down on itself, starts making excuses, starts blaming "bad breaks" or one another for what's wrong. A slump can start for one reason – a batter or pitcher may slip into some small technical flaw; a whole club may have a couple of rotten games in the field or at bat. But it can continue for quite a different reason – something in the head. And one of the things a lot of young ballplayers need to learn is how to lose without screwing up their heads. The dark hidden nightmare in Jay fans' souls is that these losing Jays are the real Jays, that they're still just an expansion club after all. But they are not. If they don't win the division this year, it will be because they are not quite yet equal to the job; the main word here is *yet*.

A final note about the slump: the Jays are, in spite of it, still a game ahead of their pace last season when, after seventy-three games, they had won forty-two; this year they have won forty-three. There are, though, a couple of differences between the seasons. (1) Their longest losing stretch last year prior to August was three games and their longest winning stretch five games. This year they have already lost five in a row twice and have rattled of bunches of seven straight wins and, a couple of times, five straight wins. They are, in a word, playing streakier ball. (2) Last

---

* Something else that may have mattered during June is that the Jays seem to be a better club on artificial turf, on which they play at home and in K.C., Minnesota, and Seattle, and where they can make better use of their speed and good defence, than on natural grass, on which the remainder of the East Division plays. This is especially true when their power is not cranked up. They played fifteen games on grass during June and won only four; on turf, in contrast, they were seven-and-four for the month. (See Chapter Thirteen.)

year, after seventy-three games, they were two games up in first place. This year they are in distant second, in the shadow of the Tigers.

Item:

• Ernie Whitt, badly cut on the leg in a collision at home with a Boston base runner, is on the disabled list until about July 1. With Geno Petralli gone, the club had to dig down to Syracuse for a backup catcher and brought up Toby Hernandez. Buck Martinez, meanwhile, has handled the bulk of the backstop work, and playing daily seems to have helped him at the plate, where he had been slumping since April. In the ten days Whitt has been out, Martinez has logged a slugging average of .571.

July 8

Today is the beginning of the All-Star break. The Jays closed out the first half with an eleven-game homestand against Oakland, California, and Seattle. While they did not set the world on fire, they did notch seven wins. Detroit, meanwhile, absorbed seven losses, so the Jays have crept up to seven gmes back – precisely where they were two months ago. The Orioles, for their part, have been playing win-one, lose-one ball and are mired pretty solidly in third place – no immediate threat to the Jays.

The old adage has it that the club that leads at the All-Star break will lead at season's end, and like a lot of old adages, sometimes this one is true and sometimes it isn't. It has suffered particular violence in the A.L. East from time to time because of the Orioles' and, in the late seventies, the Yanks' habits of pillage and rapine down the stretch. Last year, for example, the Jays were in first at the break. But the oddsmakers this year are squarely behind the Tigers to stay in front to the wire. Maybe. The Jays and their fans must hope they are wrong. The club is, at least, out of its mudhole.

Hunting for patterns in the Jays' recent homestand is not easy business. There was a soupçon of twenty-nine flavours. They did squeak out one late-inning cliffhanger, a

120

7-6 decision against the A's, in which the Jays rallied for four in the bottom of the seventh. But that was the only game of that familiar ilk; and none were decided in a last at-bats. They did, once more, leave Dave Stieb in the lurch, stuck with another 2-1 loss, also to the A's. In the three losses with which Stieb has been tagged so far this year, the Jay offence has scored precisely two runs. And they did get four fine starting outings and wins from Stieb, Alexander, Leal, and Jim Gott. Gott's, especially, was a standout, a two-hit complete game shutout of the Angels. A lot of smart money says Gott will be a whale of a pitcher some day – he is only twenty-four – and he continues to illustrate why with these occasional flashes of brilliance.

Gott was also the pitcher of record in the homestand's opener, a bent game against Oakland. The evening's tone was appropriately struck by a demure schoolgirl vocalist who sang the anthems *a cappella* and, after negotiating their jawbreaking octaves with considerable skill, rendered the final note of "O Canada" staggeringly flatly. The A's plunged the Jay crowd into a slough of despond by tallying four quick counters in the top of frame one. The Jays were fresh from their calamitous jaunt to Milwaukee, and they and their fans had hoped for a turn of fortune back on home turf.

But emotions reversed rapidly in the inning's bottom when young Oakland hurler Tim Conroy was entirely unable to make even nodding acquaintance with the strike zone. He crowded the sacks on twelve errant pitches and was two-and-oh on the fourth Jay batter when A's manager Jackie Moore bade him to a shower (even though he had thus far spun a no-hitter). The Jays squandered this chance to redress matters by converting only one of Conroy's b.b.'s to a run, leaving two on base, but the cheerfulness that had blossomed as the frustrated Oakland ballsman had tried to recall how to pitch (the cheerfulness did not include Conroy; the outing was, for him, unabated misery) seemed to restore the Jays' and the crowd's spirits. Maybe the evening could be made to turn out all right after all.

The next participant, after Conroy, evicted from the pro-ceedings was Bobby Cox, after a kinetic rhubarb with an ump in the top of the second; as Jay fortunes have waned this month, so, it seems, has Cox's patience with the Four Blind Mice. Oakland skipper Moore, not to be upstaged, was later directed from the premises after a similar differ-ence of opinion. Gott, meanwhile, settled down and pitched commendably for most of the match's duration, needing only a flourish of ninth-inning relief from Jimmy Key, who concluded the game by whiffing the final two Oakland batters on six pitches. Conroy's successors were not so successful. The Jays whacked them for a couple of homers, a couple of triples, a double, a clutch of other hits, and eight more runs; they were aided by six more Oakland walks and two errors. (Gott, for his part, was not helped by the three Jay errors.) And, lo, the losing streak was broken, a trashy but, for the Jays and their fans, salutary ball game.

Jim Clancy was less lucky than Gott. In the first match of the California set he pitched seven adequate innings, allowing only three runs, and it seemed he might turn his slump around. But in the eighth he allowed Fred Lynn and Reggie Jackson base hits, and Cox went to Dennis Lamp, who was unable to hold the fort. He got two outs on two grounders – his defence could not turn a d.p. – but a liner off his glove then loaded the bases, and a single to left drove two runs home, putting the game out of reach. Lamp is not among the Jays whose mistakes one ascribes to tender age; he is thirty-one. And his mistakes are often little ones; too often, for instance, he allows the first batter he faces to get on base. He doesn't usually commit the kinds of shockers for which the Jay pen has achieved notoriety in seasons past – the eleventh-inning homer he allowed in Fenway last month is not typical. And frequently he does do the job. But his forte is putting the ball in play, and when the ball goes in play, a lot can and sometimes does go awry. In sum, Lamp has been, though not wholly consistent, a useful addition to the pen. But he has not been – as no one really expected he would be – a total solution.

In his final start of the half Clancy ebbed back into his slump, allowing five earned runs in only a couple of innings – all on hits; he walked none – and the Jays bowed to Seattle 8-4. The following day, in the Jays' last game before the break, Gott struggled through a similarly ill-starred outing, a mere five days after his Cy Young performance against the Angels. (Young pitchers do need patience.) Meanwhile the Jay bats played dead. And so the Jays ended the half as they had started it, beat by their sibling Mariners. After eighty-four games in 1983 the Jays had won fifty and lost thirty-four. And after eighty-four games this season they have won fifty and lost thirty-four.

Items:

• Willie Upshaw concluded the half in a bad slump, batting an almost unmentionable .093 during the eleven-game homestand. Lloyd Moseby and Jesse Barfield took up some of the slack. Moseby batted .350 and slugged .775, and Barfield, who played six games in rightfield, batted .454 and slugged 1.182. His bag included a double, a triple, and five homers, and in the six games he drove in nine runs.

• The Jays will be represented in tomorrow's All-Star Game by Dave Stieb, the A.L.'s starting pitcher for the second year running, and by Damaso Garcia and Alfredo Griffin, who will back up at second base and shortstop.

Standings, A.L. East, July 9

	W	L	PCT.	GB
Detroit	57	27	.679	—
Toronto	50	34	.595	7
Baltimore	46	39	.541	11½
Boston	41	43	.488	16
Milwaukee	39	47	.453	19
New York	36	46	.439	20
Cleveland	33	49	.402	23

NINE

On the Road Again:
Bride of the
Bullpen Chainsaw Massacre

We're playing good; we're just not winning.
— Bobby Cox

The longer this goes on, the stranger whatever it is we're
hoping happens to Detroit is going to have to be.
— Buck Martinez

July 26

When the Jays are on the road, as they have been for two weeks, a circuit of the West Division, fans follow the club's fortunes mainly by radio. Baseball and radio are a good marriage, partly because of the nature of the game, an unhurried sequence of events that follows the ball from pitcher to batter to fielder. There is also a lot going on which does not follow the ball and which happens at the same time, like defensive positioning and base running tactics. But, even so, the game lends itself better to radio than, say, football, in which everything happens suddenly and all at once; it is a game which almost has to be seen first-hand – describing a football play is like trying to narrate a bar-room brawl.

Touting radio is not a whack at the tube. Baseball watched on TV does not have the immediacy of baseball watched in the ballpark, but there are features of the game that may be seen better through the camera's eye than from many park seats – a pitcher's eyes, a pitch, a batter's cut, a fielding gem. Television offers its own intimacies, and close-ups and slow motion shots and instant replays are often instructive. Fancy camerawork may, of course, be overdone. One recalls Hall of Famer and Expo commentator Duke Snider running out of comment a few years ago when his producer apparently expected him to have something useful to say about five different shots of Gary Carter dropping a high and wickedly tailing pop foul in the maw of the visitors' dugout, a tough but playable chance. After discussing the misplay through shots of Carter missing the catch from the angles of the third-base, home-plate, and leftfield cameras, Snider sat mute through a slow motion shot of Carter missing the catch from the angle of the first-base camera. When yet another shot of Carter missing the catch, a zoom from the centrefield camera, appeared, Snider observed, "I guess we're going to keep showing this until Gary gets it right."

But radio has its own advantages. For one, it involves the fan in the process of recreating the game, which may help to better understand and appreciate baseball – painting one's own pictures in the mind's eye. Television, in contrast, tends to discourage imagination. And radio is portable. It goes where one usually wants to be in baseball season, outside, where one can catch the game while tending the dandelion patch or just sitting at dusk in the yard. Too, radio can go to the cottage where, at night, one can hear not only the Jays but pull in broadcasts from as far afield as Boston, Philadelphia, and St. Louis (the Red Sox, Phils, and Cards seem to transmit particularly well to Ontario cottage country). On any one night one may find eight or ten different games on the dial.

But, at bottom, it may simply be that baseball, an old game which lends itself well to being told as a story, and radio, an old medium which can tell stories well, seem made for each other. Like box scores in the morning paper and old tattered souvenirs gathering dust on a shelf, radio is part of the game. (TV, for all it offers, isn't; it's always on the outside, looking in.) Ask fans about the best games they remember, and odds are that some of them will have been radio games.

The Jays' road trip was not quite a disaster. On second thought, maybe it was. They played fifteen games – in Oakland, Anaheim, Seattle, and K.C. – and lost eight. Meanwhile, the Tigers have streaked again – eleven and three since the All-Star break – and are once more flirting with .700. The Jays are eleven and a half games in arrears. Not good.

The really ugly stat is the Jays' record since their bout with Detroit back in June. The A.L. East since then:

	W	L	PCT	GB
Detroit	24	14	.632	—
Boston	19	17	.528	4
Baltimore	20	18	.526	4
New York	20	18	.526	4
Cleveland	20	20	.500	5
Milwaukee	20	21	.488	5½
Toronto	19	20	.487	5½

That club at the bottom is the Jays.

The press line lately has been: well, yes, the Jays are way back of the Tigers, but the Tigers are playing inspired ball (true), and the Jays still do have the third-best record in the majors (true), so the Jays are still playing pretty good ball (tricky). The Jays did have a phenomenal May, the happy epoch of the one-run ball game. They played .760 ball that month. But it was this commendable binge of wins that has otherwise kept their heads above water. Their record apart from May has been thirty-eight wins and thirty-six losses, barely more than .500 ball.

So what's wrong? Has not this tome extolled these young Jays as maybe the hottest item since fried fresh clams with a side of slaw? Has it not led the reader to believe these Jays might not ride down from the north like a horde of avenging Huns (led by Attila the Stieb) to cleave their once-derisive foes asunder? Well, yes and no. One has, in spite of a fan's partiality, tried to maintain some objectivity. But, in truth, one has pussyfooted. One has mealymouthed a bit.

There is a paradox here. It is Bobby Cox's assessment that is probably closest to the truth: "We're playing good," he averred as the road trip wound down, "we're just not winning." The Jays *are*, in most respects, "playing good." Their offence remains among the toughest in the majors. They hit .281 and slugged .523 during the losing road trip, and their b.a. is now highest in either league. (One offensive stat, in particular, catches the eye, triples, of which the Jays now have whacked fifty-two. The top three triples hitters in the league are, at the moment, Jays: Moseby, Collins, and Upshaw.) During the trip they scored seventy-five runs, an average of five a game.

Starting pitching? Stieb, Leal, Alexander, and Clancy, who seems to have pitched himself out of his slump, had a sum e.r.a. on the road trip of 3.28, and Bryan Clark started a game and allowed but a run in six innings, walking only one and chucking no wild pitches. The only starter badly roughed up in an outing was Jim Gott, and this occurred in a game in K.C. in which, as we will see, there were mitigating circumstances. Nope, no problem here. (A word about Clark. The Jays have, in effect, gone with nine pitchers to date this year, leaving first Joey McLaughlin and then Clark largely idle on the bench, not without reason. And so Clark's resurrection, if this is what his sound outing signifies – Cox used him in Seattle, Clark's old home park, perhaps an insightful stroke of psychology – augurs well for the weeks ahead. The schedule will clog next month with a clutch of rescheduled spring rainouts on the road, and the Jays will need all the pitching depth they can muster. The fact Clark is a southpaw is a nice added bonus.*)

Defence? The Jays committed ten errors during the fifteen games of the trip, not bad – their opponents committed nineteen. More to the point, they allowed their opponents only three unearned runs, only one of which mattered; they were allowed to score ten. And, again, there were occasional gems – for one, an uncanny catch by Jesse Barfield which may well have saved a game in Seattle. (Bottom of the ninth, none out, a Mariner on first, Jays ahead in the

---

* Clark's good outing in Seattle did not, it turned out, signify a resur rection. His season with the Jays was, in the end, sufficiently troubled that his future with the club is uncertain.

match by two runs. A Mariner lashes a ball deep to right-field which Barfield, coming from nowhere, snares against the alley wall. Broadcaster Tom Cheek goes momentarily bananas. "He caught the ball! He caught the ball! I can't believe it! Jesse Barfield *caught the ball!*") So, defence – no problem here either.

And put all these pieces together in a match in which the Jays are on their game, and there is no club in the majors they cannot play ball with, including the mighty Tigers. They are not, of course, always on their game. But ·they are a better ballclub than their record suggests – playing good, as Cox puts it, but not winning. So what's wrong?

Mm. As acknowledged, one has pussyfooted; skated around a delicate question; turned, if not a blind eye, a carefully blinkered one, hoping that somehow, when the chips were down, it would all turn out all right. But it has not turned out all right. Fairy tale endings do not happen in baseball. Make a mistake, baseball will rip your heart out. You can't fool it, can't bluff yourself out of a position of weakness like you can with a busted flush. We are talking, of course, about the Jay bullpen. The cat is out of the bag.

Oh, they did have better moments. Roy Jackson tallied three saves, and each of the others – Lamp, Key, Acker, Clark – did, here or there, at least an outing's sound service. Last night, for example, Jim Acker held the Royals in check for four tough innings and Clark held them for a fifth while the Jay offence flailed away at trying to put across one of the runners it got on base and unknot a tied score. It was a game that mattered. The Jays were seven-and-seven on the trip by then, so the outcome meant the difference between returning home with a bag above or below .500. The Jay offence failed to tally, and in the bottom of the thirteenth the Royals bunched a single, a sac. bunt, and another single for the g.w.r.b.i. But if it was the pen that kept the Jays in this game, it was the pen, too, that allowed K.C. to lock the score in the first place. In the bottom of the eighth – Jays 4,

Royals 3 – Jimmy Key had thrown a consecutive and un-characteristic pair of wild pitches which permitted a runner on first to become a runner on third. He scored a moment later when Key surrendered a double to George Brett.

Still, the game did not much rankle. If Key had gaffed, he had at least not tossed the game in the trash bin. The Jay offence had ample time to do something remedial, and one pitch, cheap single, runner picked off one way or the other, and the Jays might have squeaked the match out. No, it had been four other games that rankled – a game in Oak-land, which the Jays were leading 4-1, in which the pen allowed the A's six runs in the seventh; a game in Anaheim, which the Jays led 2-1, in which the pen allowed the Angels a run in the sixth and three in the seventh; a game in Seattle, tied 1-1, in which the pen allowed the Mariners eight runs – *eight* – in the seventh; a game in K.C., which the Jays were leading 5-3, in which the pen allowed the Royals a run in the seventh and five in the eighth.

This latter game, the first of the K.C. series and game one of a twin-bill, seemed to break the Jays' heart. They had, in spite of clunkers one, two, and three above, left the west coast at seven wins and four losses and needed only a split in the four games in K.C. to come home with a .600 record on the trip. And they were already five-and-oh against the Royals this season. But they did not get the split. They lost all four games, starting with this fourth savaging of the pen in twelve days. It was in the second half of the twin-bill that Gott was mauled, a game the Jays played like whipped curs. One of the difficulties with a capricious pen is it can get a whole team down in the dumps and looking over its shoulder. These gaffes by the pen were not one-run mis-takes. They were blowouts. And they were committed in roughly equal measure by each of the pen's inhabitants: team efforts. They were a sequel to the events of late 1983 – the Bride of the Bullpen Chainsaw Massacre.

So it goes, and no hard feelings. Lord knows, these guys try as hard to play good ball as they try the patience; they don't *want* to get shelled. No boos here. One could sure as hell do no better oneself. There are times when the best hitters in the league – Murray, Rice, Brett, Winfield – cannot hit squat off Lamp or Acker or Key or Jackson. The problem is the other times. You can play .500 ball with an iffy pen – not incompetent, just inconsistent – and with starters, hitters, and fielders like the Jays', you can maybe even play .600 ball. But it is not likely you can win a pennant, especially not when the club you have to beat is burning down the house the way the Tigers are this season.

One looks around the leagues and sees Dan Quisenberry in K.C. (twenty-seven saves and four wins so far this year, including a couple of saves and a win against the Jays this week), Bruce Sutter in St. Louis (twenty-three saves and three wins), Al Holland in Philadelphia (twenty-two saves and four wins), and Bill Caudill in Oakland (twenty-one saves – the entire Jay relief corps has logged twenty-one saves this year – and eight wins). Each of the hot clubs – the Tigers, Mets, Padres, Cubs – has an ace in the pen: Willie Hernandez, Jesse Orosco, Rick Gossage, Lee Smith.*

These are baseball's Mighty Mice, the guys who come on the job when the mortgage is on the line and little brother's been beat up and sweet Bessie Sue is tied to the railroad tracks. Oh, they can be beaten, every once in a while. But usually they're not. And just having one of them shelling nuts in the pen can give another club the heebie-jeebies. You know you'd better do damage early, because if you are still goofing around by inning seven. . . . And one knows, *knows*, if the Jays had one of these guys, they would be climbing the Tigers' backs. And if the Jays had one of these guys and if Jim Clancy had not disenjoyed a month's indisposition – and if *ifs* and *buts* were candies and nuts, we'd all have a hell of a Christmas. (For the record, the conspicuous absence of Rollie Fingers from the catalogue of relief aces above is not accidental. The dean of firemen is

---

* These were, in the end, the four clubs whose records bettered the Jays' this year.

back on the disabled list, this time with lower back trouble –
again, his career may be threatened.)

Bobby Cox responded to his pen's misadventures vs. the
West with an uncharacteristic public whack at one of his
ballplayers, Jimmy Key, who, Cox said, had served up a
"stupid" pitch to Reggie Jackson (which pitch Jackson took
downtown to tie Lou Gehrig on the all-time h.r. list: 493,
thirteenth overall). One can count on one's fingers the
number of times Cox has disparaged a Jay to the press in
his years in Toronto, and that he did so was less a measure
of annoyance with Key, of whom he must know he has
been asking a lot, than of frustration at the pen's work generally. A few days later, in the wake of the K.C. disaster,
Cox announced the rechristening of Jim Gott as Goose
Gott: the club's fireballing fifth starter would move to the
pen as short man, an experiment that has been floated but
not tried before. It was, in fact, Cox's second adjustment of
the pen; immediately after the All-Star break, without announcement, he had switched Dennis Lamp's and Roy
Jackson's roles as short man and set-up man. Gott and
Jackson may now make Cox look like a genius. Or they
may make him look like a guy who is trying to jerryrig a
silk ear from a sow's purse.*

It is useful to remember at times like these that, apart
from last season, the Jays have never been anywhere but
buried deep in the basement at this point in the schedule,
useful to remember that their evolution as an expansion
club has been commendable. (There is, of course, no corollary that they will therefore continue to get better. One
need look no farther than Montreal to see an expansion
club which, apparently on the eve of dynastic domination
of its division and once but a pitch away from the World
Series, has stumbled back to the second division as a consequence of a succession of appallingly boneheaded

---

* The returns were mixed. Jackson's second half was not as strong as
  his first, and Gott endured some pointed on-the-job training. But
  each did some good work, too.

management decisions, crippling injuries, and jumbo bad breaks.) And if the Jays have not yet improved on their record of last season – after ninety-nine games they stood last year and stand this year at fifty-seven wins and forty-two losses – there remains enough time to do so, maybe even take a run at Detroit. The Jays' road trip this month is instructive about why the Tigers have opened up their portly lead. The Jays and Tigers have roughly equal records at home. The difference is that the Tigers' road record has been almost as good, while the Jays, out of town, have struggled:

	Home				Road			
	W	L	PCT.	GB	W	L	PCT.	GB
Detroit	34	14	.708	—	34	16	.680	—
Toronto	34	15	.694	½	23	27	.460	11

In any case, the old chestnut that a pennant contender must split on the road and win two out of three at home is inapplicable in a season when the frontrunner is winning two out of three ubiquitously.

Can the Jays, at this juncture, really hope to take on the Tigers? Sure. Why not? They are certainly in no worse shape than the 1914 Boston Braves who, in mid-July, were fifteen games back and in the cellar and won the N.L. flag by ten-plus games. Or the 1951 New York Giants who were thirteen and a half games back on August 11 and finished the season in a dead heat with the Dodgers (then won a three-game playoff series; it was the year of Bobby Thomson's legendary home run). Or the 1978 New York Yankees who, in mid-July, were fourteen games behind the Red Sox and also forced and won a post-season playoff. But perhaps the most instructive example for the Jays is the 1969 Miracle Mets, an expansion club also in its eighth season, who trailed by nine and a half games on August 14 and went on to write expansion-club history. (The club the

Mets overtook that year was the Cubbies, and it now appears this season's race in the N.L. East may come down to the same two teams. This sort of recurrence is not uncommon in baseball – for instance, should the Cubs exact revenge from the Mets for 1969 and then win the N.L. pennant, they may well find themselves pitted against the same club that beat them the last time, 1945, they played in the World Series, the Tigers.*)

But what these clubs and the others in baseball's history who have come from deep in a hole to win a pennant have done is perform stunningly down the stretch. The 1914 Braves won thirty-four of their last forty-four games, the 1951 Giants won fifty-two of sixty-three, the 1978 Yanks won forty-eight of sixty-eight, and the 1969 Mets won thirty-eight of forty-eight. And such heroics alone were not enough to guarantee anything; the clubs ahead of them also took headers. Not only must the Jays here on out play piranha baseball, the Tigers must do a dive from their current arithmetic. No, don't bet the farm on it, but hope is not utterly off the wall – there is precedent. As Buck Martinez has remarked, however, the longer the Jays postpone their move, the more catastrophically will the Tigers have to collapse to be caught. Detroit is playing better ball at the moment than all but a handful of clubs in the game's history, so odds are they will suffer at least modest slippage. But whether they will take the pratfall the Jays may require is another story.

Of course, this sort of reckoning of the unlikely calculus of a Jay dash to the pennant is based in the blithesome premise that Gott, Lamp, Jackson, *et al.* will perform like Quis, Goose, and Sutter down the stretch and that the other Jays will play as well as they have to date or better. Otherwise, Jay pennant hopes for this year will without doubt have had the biscuit.

---

* The Cubs knocked the Mets out of the race in a series of head-to-head matches in August and September. But they then fumbled the N.L. flag to the Padres and did not get a crack at Detroit.

Okay, guys. Go get 'em.

Items:

- Damaso Garcia was twice forced to the bench on the road trip by beanings – the Jays lead the majors so far in hit batsmen – and Alfredo Griffin subbed in his place and played good second base. And Tony Fernandez, at short in several games, is living up to his minor league raves. The kid can play ball.

- Willie Upshaw has emerged from his slump. He batted .383 on the road trip and raised his season average back over .300. And Rance Mulliniks, whose season started slowly, has found his stroke; he hit .394 and slugged .667 on the road trip. (Mulliniks came to the majors as a California Angel and was traded to the Royals in 1979 in the same deal that brought Willie Aikens from California to K.C. But with George Brett and U.L. Washington holding down the left side of the Royal infield, there was not much work for Mulliniks except as a utilityman, and he was happy to come to Toronto where he has had a chance to play more regularly. He has a clean, compact stroke and hits line drives with regularity. His .311 b.a. currently leads the club.) Finally, George Bell has fallen on hard times, hitting only .196 on the road trip; his average has dropped from .314 to .295 since the All-Star break.

Standings, A.L. East, July 26

	W	L	PCT.	GB
Detroit	68	30	.694	—
Toronto	57	42	.576	11½
Baltimore	55	45	.550	14
Boston	50	46	.521	17
New York	46	51	.474	21½
Milwaukee	45	55	.450	24
Cleveland	42	55	.433	25½

TEN

Revenge of the Demon Blue Jays

All baseball fans believe in miracles. The question is, how *many* do you believe in?
— John Updike

August 2

The Jays returned home from the west for six days of pretty good ball, a pair of three-game sets against the Rangers and Royals. All but one of the matches remained unsettled until the late frames; no laughers here.

Game one belonged to Charlie Hough, his third start of the season against the Jays and his second win. The Jays do not seem able to do much with Hough's peripatetic knuckler. Hough's trouble in the one match he lost, played in Toronto in May, was not that the Jays roughed him up but that he untypically could not get his mercurial pitch under control and issued a batch of walks and wild pitches.

Hough, who may log nearly twenty wins for a losing club this year, pitched ten-plus seasons of sound relief for the Dodgers before his sale in 1980 to Texas, where he converted to starting. He reckons he has a good five, maybe ten years left in his rubbery arm. He is thirty-six, so this sentiment may seem unrealistic; but maybe not. The knuckler is more the coinage of craft than physical effort, and its practitioners often enjoy longer careers than hurlers of more arm-wrenching stuff. Hoyt Wilhelm's longevity was in main part because of his knuckler, and the durable Phil Niekro, the current doyen of the butterfly ball, is enjoying, at forty-five, an excellent season for the Yanks this year. (Niekro, an A.L. All-Star last month, offered a memorable baseball image when he was caught by the TV camera late in the game sitting alone at one end of the dugout. He was warmed up and wore a jacket and, around his neck, a towel; silvery hair slipped from under the brim of his cap. His eyes were riveted on the game, and he was smacking a ball impatiently in his mitt, like any little-leaguer eager to get out there and *play*. "Lemme in, coach! Lemme in!" Regrettably, and to his disgruntlement, he was not let in.)

Only once in the match against Hough did the Jays seriously threaten to rally. Dave Collins, Alfredo Griffin, and Lloyd Moseby knocked third-inning singles, tying the game at one and putting runners on first and third with one out. The Texas ace suddenly seemed hittable, and the next batter was Willie Upshaw, one of the few Jays who has been able to get at Hough in the past. It was a good moment for theft of second – Moseby would move into scoring position, and the Rangers' chance for a d.p. would be removed – and Moseby leaned away from first. Hough threw over to draw him back, which Moseby did easily; Hough's move was lackadaisical. The pantomime was repeated again, a third time, and a fourth, Moseby moving slightly farther away from the bag with each throw and each time getting back with no problem. Hough peered at the plate – mm, Upshaw – and at Moseby, and at the plate, and *wham*. Hough showed Moseby his *good* move – it is one of the best in the league – and Moseby was hung out to dry. Two down. Hough dispatched Upshaw on a grounder to second, end of inning.

In the sixth Texas got to Doyle Alexander for a single by Mickey Rivers, a triple by Gary Ward, and an s.f., and that, pretty much, was the ball game. Hough and Alexander both pitched good complete games, but Alexander made one more mistake than Hough, Ward's bookended triple, which was enough to tilt the match's balance.

Luis Leal started game two of the set and was hampered by a badly stiff neck. He lasted less than three innings – his first rotten outing of the season – during which he allowed five walks, a couple of singles, two homers, and three Ranger runs; it was a marvel they didn't score more. Still, all was not lost. The Jays struck back with homers by Upshaw and Whitt and led 4-3 after four. Jim Acker replaced Leal and pitched a pair of good frames, and Roy Jackson replaced Acker and pitched a good one. But Jackson started the seventh by issuing a walk and allowing a single, at which juncture Cap'n Cox made his third trek of the evening to the mound. Onto the field stepped the Jays' brand new stopper, Jim Gott, and somewhere above, no doubt, Firpo Marberry told the archangel chorus to pipe down for a moment and leaned a little closer to his celestial radio.

Gott (1) pitched three good innings and (2) learned a crucial lesson about working out of the pen. But the three good innings occurred only after he had surrendered base hits on three pitches to the first two Rangers he faced, good for the tying and go-ahead runs. And the lesson he learned was not to adjourn from the bullpen mound until he is quite sure he is ready to confront real batters. He admitted in the locker room afterward that he had been too eager to get into the game and probably should have dallied a moment longer warming up. The Rangers' tally was left unanswered, and the game went into the books the Jays' sixth consecutive loss.

In the final match of the set Dave Stieb and Danny Darwin battled grimly for seven-plus innings to a meagre 2-1 Texas advantage, the kind of pitching duel that lingers in the mind. Stieb allowed a couple of doubles for a Ranger run in the first but then did not permit a base runner, apart from one hit batsman, until the eighth, when Texas bunched three singles for another run. And Darwin did not allow a hit until Rick Leach nubbed a two-out single in the fifth. Both hurlers worked quickly, painted the black, and stayed ahead of hitters, and both were assisted by some occasionally marvelous glovework. Moseby, Rance Mulliniks, and Damaso Garcia made particularly pretty plays for the Jays.

Darwin seemed to have lost nothing as he went to work in the eighth; he whiffed Collins on three rapid strikes. But the Jays were not ready to roll over. Moseby whacked a double. Ranger skipper Doug Rader now directed Darwin to pass Upshaw to first, to set up the double play and to get at Willie Aikens, a baldly patent effrontery to the once-feared slugger (i.e., deliberately putting the go-ahead run on base in order to have a righty pitch to the lefty Aikens). But, in truth, Aikens has not been a ball of fire since joining the roster in May. He has done some damage – six homers, thirty-plus ribbies – but inconsistently, and his b.a. entering the game was a bare .220. It may not be until next year that Aikens fulfils the Jays' hopes. And Rader's instructions to pitch around Upshaw were doubly insulting to Aikens because the Texas manager had employed precisely this tactic two innings earlier to good effect. With one out and Collins aboard in the sixth, Moseby had tripled – the tying run was home, the go-ahead run at third – and Rader had similarly ordered Upshaw walked to get at Aikens. Aikens had whiffed, his third K of the game, and Moseby and Upshaw ended up l.o.b.'s.

But Rader's ploy did not work twice. Aikens now pecked a single through the infield, scoring Moseby, and the floodgates opened. Before the frame ended, the Jays had rallied for five runs and Darwin was routed to the showers. Aikens' small but decisive hit won him a standing ovation from the fans who, a moment earlier, had been booing – not at Aikens but at Darwin and the Texas bench for refusing to pitch, a second time, to the Jays' clean-up man; Jays fans like to see Upshaw bat. Stieb polished off Texas in the top of the ninth, and a game was finally won.

Texas moved on, and K.C. moved in and, the following evening, rapped Jim Clancy for four runs in inning one, a handicap the Jays were unable to overcome – the one match of the homestand that was not, for at least seven innings, a squeaker. So Clancy is again a question mark. Has he really recovered, as seemed on the road trip, from his slump? If he goes back in a mudhole, the Jays are in terminal trouble.

In game two of the K.C. set the Royals gobbled three runs out of Alexander in the second, but the Jays got them back in their half of the frame and added two more in the third. So matters stood through six. Alexander then bogged himself down – a walk, an out, another walk. Due up was George Brett, and Cox yanked Alexander and brought in Jimmy Key. The crowd was understandably restive about the move, not so much booing it as debating it among themselves, ten or eleven thousand animated and concurrent arguments over peanuts and beer about whether Cox ought to be staying with Alexander rather than reaching into the Jays' boobytrapped pen. Key vindicated his skipper by doing the job; Brett popped to centre. Cox now replaced Key with Roy Lee Jackson to pitch to Hal McRae – more murmuring from the crowd, but less anxiously. Jackson whiffed McRae on four pitches.

In the eighth the clubs swapped homers (Frank White, George Bell), and so the game went into the top of the ninth, Jays 6, Royals 4. Jackson got two quick outs and had to retire only Brett to terminate matters. He did not. Brett doubled. Jackson now had to retire only McRae to terminate matters. He did not. McRae doubled Brett home, and the match became a one-run ball game in the final ups with a runner on second and a pretty good hitter, Dane Iorg (Garth's brother), coming to bat. Time for The Stopper. Cox hooked Jackson and dispatched Gott to the mound, and, hot damn, Gott did the job, retiring Iorg on an easy grounder. Thus did Goose Gott notch his first ever major or minor league save.

However much baseball one sees, there is always something one hasn't seen – the d.p., for instance, which the Jays turned in inning five of the final game against K.C. Leal, after his ignominious attempt to play hurt four days earlier, seemed at first his old self. Apart from a solo homer the Royals had little luck with him through four. The Jays answered the run a couple of outs later, and the game went into the fifth locked at one. Now, however, Leal abruptly seemed vulnerable, not quite making his pitches, and a pair of Royals, White and Onix Concepcion, led off with singles.

Next up was Willie Wilson, who took a shot at bunting the runners over, didn't do it, then swung away on a pitch, apparently trying to drive the ball to the right side and move the runners that way. Leal's pitch, however, had nice movement on it, and Wilson managed only to beat it into the dirt in front of the plate where it dribbled along the first-base line. Wilson had legged his way hardly halfway to the bag when one concluded despondently that K.C. now had the damn sacks full; Wilson goes from home to first, remember, faster than any runner in the league. But wait; the play wasn't over. Buck Martinez barreled furiously from behind the plate, pounced on the ball, and pegged a rope to Upshaw that arrived a bare sliver of a second before Wilson crossed the bag. All right! But wait; the play wasn't over. Leal, transfixed by his catcher's heroics, failed to cover home, his job in this situation, and White, coming around third, saw the unguarded plate only ninety feet away and never stopped running. Jay third-sacker Garth Iorg, however (prompted, he said later, by voices from the Jay bench), saw the unmanned plate, too, and a footrace was on. Iorg arrived a step ahead of White, took Upshaw's peg – a perfect leading throw, delivered when Iorg was still coming down the line – and tagged White on the hip as he slid. The ump pumped his fist, d.p., so far as anyone could recall, a unique d.p.: G2-3-5-covering-home.

Leal was, however, still not out of the fire. Concepcion had gone to third, Leal now issued a walk, and Brett drove a sharp liner to short centre, dropping, dropping – into Moseby's glove. Running at full tilt, the Jay centrefielder snagged the ball a few inches off the turf, and the inning and threat were over.

In his subsequent frames Leal again turned tough, and later Jimmy Key was once more summoned, as he had been the night before, to dispatch George Brett, which he did handily. Again, Brett was the only batter he faced. Ernie Whitt whacked a two-run dinger, and Jim Gott pitched a couple of innings of good relief for his second save in two nights. The Jays had another game in the win column and a three-three split of the homestand.

But .500 ball will not help the Jays much in catching the Tigers. Though Detroit did falter this week, the Jays picked up only a single game in the standings – a chance lost.

Tomorrow, what appears to be the battle for second place will begin when the Jays journey to Baltimore for a three-game set. And next week the Orioles play four matches in Toronto. The O's have lately been winning slightly more than the Jays and are now only two and a half games in the Jays' wake.

August 6

The Jays arrived in Baltimore amid indecorous scoffing in the local press about the Jays' inconstant pen, the slumps Garth Iorg and Buck Martinez are enduring, the tribulations of Willie Aikens. They are not scoffing today.

Recollections of the matches – the Jays swept the set – blur cheerfully in the mind. Oh, some moments do stand out clearly. Jim Clancy pitched a dandy complete game, and in one of the matches Dave Collins stole four bases as the Jays in all stole seven, a new club high. In the same game Cliff Johnson knocked his nineteenth career pinch-hit home run, a new major league record. Noteworthy work was done by the Baltimore press's scoffees. Buck Martinez smacked a two-run homer, Aikens drilled a three-run homer, Iorg tallied a pair of r.b.i.'s, and the Jay pen – Lamp, Jackson, Gott, and Key pitched – allowed a single run in nine innings' work. But more than these separate memories there remains an impression of the team as a whole, hard-edged, tight, playing remorseless ball.

It was in the field, particularly, that the Jays bettered the O's, which will trouble Oriole fans, accustomed to a bed-rock of solid glovework on their club. Weakness here may signify a decline of the club generally.* Their hitting, too, is off – they are second-last in the league in b.a. and down in homers. Only the pitching, second-best in the league (to Detroit), is of the calibre of World Series champs, which, for the moment, the O's still are. So maybe that championship last season *was* just a residue of the Weaver era; maybe Weaver *was* the guts of the Orioles' winning ways.

Still, one would not yet place any bets on it. The O's have

* The Orioles' defensive lapses in the set were only momentary. They did, in the end, once again lead the A.L. in fielding.

been too good for too long – they are used to winning – and they have in Eddie Murray and Cal Ripken the two finest players at their positions in the majors. And though Weaver is absent, the old Oriole organization still remains. But with Jim Palmer gone and Ken Singleton apparently nearing retirement (he is batting .216, and Baltimore management is scouting for a new d.h.), and with the younger players in the lineup so far failing to pull their weight (they are barely batting their weight), the O's have slipped. Now, after their throttling by the Jays, they are only a game in front of the Red Sox and a game and a half in front of the Yanks. Sure, they may still execute one of their red-hot stretch drives. But they are, for the moment, back on their heels and playing lacklustre ball, not good enough to have escaped a beating this weekend at the hands of their old patsies on their own home turf. The Demon Blue Jays have had a measure of revenge. Four games with the O's do, however, remain to be played in Toronto this week; maybe one should not count one's Orioles before they hatch.

While the Jays were in Baltimore, the Royals were in Detroit pounding the Tigers silly, four games to none; and a couple of the scores – 9-6, 9-5 – suggest that the Tabbies' mound staff is finally falling on hard times. The distance between the Jays and Tigers has closed to eight games.

August 10
Kippered in the heart of Texas.

If Detroit does go on to win this thing and the tale is then told that the Tigers were just too hot to handle this season, built up too big a lead too quickly, then hung tough enough that it was impossible to catch them, don't buy it. The Jays did have a chance.

The Tigers travelled to Boston this week for a set that included back-to-back doubleheaders, a consequence of spring rain outs. Boston won three of five games – again, the scores of Detroit's losses suggest trouble on the mound: 10-2, 12-7, 8-0. And so the Jays, playing three matches in

Texas, might have picked up two games in the standings, which would have lodged them six back. Six is a magic number here; the Jays have six games remaining with the Tigers this year. While they have no control over how Detroit fares in their other matches, they do at least have it in their grasp to determine the outcome of these six. This arithmetic, however, assumes the Jays would have swept their three matches with the Rangers, and they won only one. Coming away from their happy weekend in Baltimore, they slumped – not badly; just enough to lose a couple.

There is a pattern here. Each time this year the Jays have won a clutch of vital games, they have subsequently, nearly immediately, done a header. After their three-game April sweep of the Orioles in Toronto, they went belly-up for three matches against California. Following their defeat of the Tigers and three-game sweep of the Red Sox in June, they went into a two-and-eight mudhole. And in the midst of the Tiger series they dropped three to the Yanks. Then this week they left Baltimore riding high and were struck down by the lowly Rangers. This kind of streakiness is one other characteristic of a young ballclub which is on its way but is not quite there.

It was, again, partly the bullpen which let down in Texas. In one of their losses the Jays led 4-3 entering the bottom of the eighth, at which point Roy Jackson and Jim Gott surrendered two runs. Final score, 5-4. In the other loss, after Jimmy Key had pitched two good innings (no hits, no walks, no runs), Dennis Lamp allowed Texas a counter in the bottom of the tenth of a 6-6 tie. And because the pen is a club's final line of defence on the road (at home a club at least gets another ups), the relief corps' failings were the most immediately conspicuous here. But there were other problems, too. In frame six of the first loss the Jays lodged runners at first and third with none out, then left them there as Upshaw, Aikens, and Bell made easy outs. In the same frame's bottom Luis Leal allowed a single, then walked two batters to clog the sacks and set the table for a pair of

Ranger runs. And in the second loss Dave Stieb allowed Texas a five-run inning. No, the pen was not the only problem.

It would be wrong-headed at a moment like this to come down on the ballplayers, wrong-headed and out of line. The Jays have won seven of their past ten games, and every one of the Texas goats – Jackson, Gott, Lamp, Stieb, Upshaw, Aikens, Bell, Leal – helped win those seven matches.

So maybe one is expecting a miracle. Maybe the Tigers can't be caught. And you cannot very well fault the damn ballplayers if, at this point of the season, they can't work a miracle. *(Boo! Ya bum! Ya can't turn water into wine!)* Still, baseball fans believe in miracles; they're part of the game. And every now and then, they do happen.

Bobby Cox made a couple of interesting lineup moves on the Texas trip.

For one, he sat down Willie Aikens as his lefty d.h. and played Cliff Johnson both ways. Johnson hits righties nearly as well as southpaws – since joining the Jays, .281 vs. lefties, .277 vs. righties; his run-production stats are comparable. And Johnson has been on a tear since the All-Star break, batting .350 and whacking six homers in sixty at-bats. Johnson responded to his skip's stratagem by pounding one of the longest home runs ever hit in Arlington Stadium.

Cox's more intriguing move was in the infield. Rance Mulliniks was forced to the bench by back spasms this week, and Garth Iorg remains in a slump. So Cox reached into his bag of tricks for a couple of games and plucked out a sub. third-sacker who has been batting .339, slugging .554, and playing impeccable defense, albeit, at another position, since the All-Star break – one Tony Fernandez. The kid handled his new assignment with competence. This particular decoding of the Griffin/Garcia/Fernandez riddle is not a brand new light bulb that flashed on over Cox's head. The notion of giving Fernandez some work at third – he has not played the position before – has been cautiously floated in past. And, on the topic of third-basemen, Kelly Gruber, down in Syracuse, is chewing up triple-A pitching.

Three final notes:

• In the Texas game the Jays did win their pitcher was Jim Clancy, who again acquitted himself well, hurling eight good innings. Every time Clancy pitches soundly, his slump is farther behind him.

• In their final three innings against the Rangers this season, the Jays faced Joey McLaughlin. The score was 5-1 Jays – it was Clancy's game – when McLaughlin took the mound. In his first inning he walked Ernie Whitt, then allowed Fernandez to tag him for a two-run homer. Otherwise, he closed the Jays down. Jays 7, Texas 2.*

• In April, the Rangers became the first A.L. club against whom the Jays were playing better than .500 ball over their eight-season history. Their two-and-four record against Texas since the All-Star break, however, gives them a six-six split of their season series, so they have dropped back again to .500 against Texas overall (forty-five wins, ditto losses).

Standings, A.L. East, August 10

	W	L	PCT.	GB
Detroit	74	41	.643	—
Toronto	64	47	.577	8
Baltimore	60	53	.531	13
Boston	59	54	.522	14
New York	58	54	.518	14½
Cleveland	47	65	.420	25½
Milwaukee	48	67	.417	26

* McLaughlin's stats with Texas for the season were two wins, a loss, no saves, and a 4.40 e.r.a. in about thirty innings' work.

ELEVEN

The Search for the Perfect Ball Game

That's the great joy of baseball. Its images are so clear,
moments so memorable, they last forever.
— Alison Gordon

August 14

Part of a fan's business is the search for the perfect ball game, a Platonic ideal, the ball game all other ball games try to imitate. The fan stalks it city to city, April to autumn, season to season. It won't, of course, ever be found. But in the process of looking for it one comes across some pretty good baseball.

The Jays and Orioles had their last meeting of the season this weekend in Toronto, four plums. Had the games been the end of the schedule, it would have been okay. One came away from the set with enough baseball memories to last through the coldest, snowiest, longest winter. It is hard to imagine thirty-six innings of much better ball.

Oh, the games didn't mean a whole lot. No one's position in the A.L. East race altered, though the O's did, in the midst of the set, drop to fourth for a day. The games were split two-two, so both clubs lost a notch and a half in the standings to the Tigers, who were three-and-oh for the weekend. But whether the games meant anything beyond themselves doesn't much matter. They were better than that.

Pitching was, for both sides, remarkable. Five complete games were hurled – the bullpens, between them, logged less than six innings' labour – and only twenty-one runs (nineteen earned) were scored. The pitchers did, now and then, work themselves into jams but they nearly always dodged the bullet.

Fielding was almost as impeccable and often decisive. Had any one of innumerable plays gone the other way, the weekend might have turned out very differently. There were only four d.p.'s, but each was critical to the flow of the game in which it occurred (although none of the d.p.'s changed an outcome; each was logged – three by the Baltimores, one by the Jays – by that match's losing side). There were four errors, but three were of no consequence. The only Oriole E.'s occurred on consecutive attempts by a hurler (Mike Boddicker) to pick off a Jay runner (Dave Collins) who, for all that, was left on base. One of two Jays miscues, by Tony Fernandez, learning the vicissitudes of the hot corner, had no ultimate ill effect. The second Jay error, however, did matter – a gaffe by Alfredo Griffin on a routine peg which put aboard the first runner in a game-breaking Oriole rally. You do not, it will be recalled, give the Orioles four-out innings.

And the offence, such as did occur, was startling and theatrical. The winning run in each game was the consequence of a homer, the set's only four homers. Two of the h.r.'s – one by each club – were logged early, and the opposing club tried and failed for the remaining frames to claw its way back. And two – again, one by each club – were logged late, each the decisive stroke in its match. There was also a fifth noteworthy clout, a bases-loaded triple by the A.L.'s ace clutch hitter, Eddie Murray, which turned the set around. Prior to Murray's triple the set had belonged to the Jays; after it, it belonged to the O's.

Doyle Alexander and Dennis Martinez each threw three-hit complete games in the first match, a game the Jays won with speed, scoring twice on the legs of their rabbits. With two out in the bottom of the third, Tony Fernandez knocked a liner to middling right-centre which Oriole centrefielder Al Bumbry ill-advisedly tried to snare on the fly. The ball bounced just past his reach and skittered to the wall, and anyone who had watched Fernandez's base-running exploits since he joined the Jays knew immediately what was about to happen, an inside-the-park homer, no contest. Once the ball was past Bumbry, the only way the O's could have stopped Fernandez from scoring was shoot him in the foot.

Later, Martinez made his only two real mistakes. He (1) walked Dave Collins and, after Collins had stolen second and gone to third on a groundout, (2) uncorked a wild pitch allowing Collins to score. But Martinez's carelessness here

Baseball Scorecard

	1	2	3	4	5	6	7	8	9	10	R	H	E	LB
ORIOLES	0	0	0	0	0	0	0	0	0		0	3	0	4
JAYS	0	0	1	0	0	0	1	0	-		2	3	0	1

Orioles

#	Player	Pos	1	2	3	4	5	6	7	8	9	10
1	Bumbry	8	43			43	K				-	
2	Ford	DH	K			-			7	8		
3	Ripken	6	53			5F			•=	9		
4	Murray	3		7		K			43	3!		
5	Gross	5		8			53		8			
6	Young	9		K			3	w				
7	Roenicke	7			1		7L		1			
8	Dauer / Nolan (8) / Sakata (8F)	4 / PH / 4			13			53	↗			
9	Dempsey / Singleton(8) / Rayford(8F)	2 / PH / 2			K			↗	8			
	R											
	H					1			1	1		
	LB					1			1	1	1	

IP — D.Martinez 8

Jays

#	Player	Pos	1	2	3	4	5	6	7	8	9	10
1	Garcia	4	4		7			8				
2	Collins	7	8			3			•S (wp) w			
3	Moseby	8	13			3			43			
4	Upshaw	3		1F		6			3F			
5	Aikens	DH		x -			5!		53			
6	Bell	9		DP 163			K		•=			
7	Mulliniks / Iorg (9F)	5 / 5			43		43			3		
8	Whitt	2				K		9D		x·P		
9	Fernandez	6			⊜			63		DP 13!		
	R				1				1			
	H			1	1				1			
	LB								1			

IP — Alexander 9

151

did not really matter. Fernandez's homer alone was suffi-
cient margin for the Jays, because the Orioles could not
score even one run against Alexander. The Jays' veteran
righty was in utter control, allowing only four base runners,
never more than one an inning, only one who got past first.

The final half-innings were each punctuated by defensive dramatics. In the bottom of the eighth George Bell
doubled and went to third on a groundout. The Orioles, not
wanting matters to get any farther out of hand, elected to
pass Ernie Whitt and create a chance for a double play.
Fernandez, the next batter, took a pitch, then cracked a
shot back through the box that Martinez barely snared; he
threw to first to nail Whitt, who had broken toward second.
It was not quite the d.p. the O's had in mind, but it would
do. In the top of the ninth Alexander allowed a lead-off
single to the speedy Bumbry and had to pitch through the
heart of the Oriole order, with a man aboard, to get out of
the game. With some help from Willie Upshaw, he managed. He retired Dan Ford and Cal Ripken on flies, and
Upshaw then snagged a vicious liner off the bat of Murray
for out three. Had Murray's whack gone through, Bumbry
would have scored, and Murray would have ended up at
least on second, more likely third. When it was over, one
just sat a few moments and let the rhythms echo and the
images settle.

This first intense game was just an overture for the
matches to come. In game two Luis Leal allowed the O's
some base runners early but was able to extricate himself
before real damage was done (a different kind of tension
than that offered by Alexander's nearly perfect stuff in game
one – less artful but more palpitating). The Jays, meanwhile,
notched an inch-by-inch run on the sequence of a single
by Rance Mulliniks, a walk, a sac., a hit batsman, and a sac.
fly, but otherwise they could do almost nothing with the
stunning stuff of young Baltimore hurler Storm Davis. Davis,
who is twenty-two, is currently the only starter in the league
pitching better than Dave Stieb.

Baseball scorecard

			1	2	3	4	5	6	7	8	9	10	R	H	E	LB
	ORIOLES		0	0	0	0	2	0	0	0	0		2	7	0	10
	JAYS		0	0	1	0	0	0	0	0	2		3	7	0	6

#	Player	Pos	1	2	3	4	5	6	7	8	9	10
1	Young	9	7F	W	K	8				W		
2	Shelby	8	K	5F	③ =		13		3			
3	Ripken	6	W	—	T —				63			
4	Murray	3	—	31!	P				—			
5	Gross	5	9		5	63			X64 W			
6	Ford	DH		K	43		53		K			
7	Roenicke	7		K	53		3F		3F			
8	Dauer	4		8	② =	63			FC			
9	Dempsey / Rayford (9F)	2 / 2		8	63		4		⅄			
		R			2							
		H	1	1	3		2					
		LB	2	2	2		3	1				

				IP
	Davis			8+

#	Player	Pos	1	2	3	4	5	6	7	8	9	10
1	Garcia	4	13	H	53				63			
2	Collins	7	4!3	5F 8		4			9			
3	Moseby	8	13	8		X			—			
4	Upshaw	3		3	K	DP 6!3			3			
5	Aikens / Leach (7)	DH / PR		8	9				W	⑥-		
6	Bell	9		9	⅄				8	①!		
7	Mulliniks	5		②-	43				X64 —			
8	Whitt	2		W	K				4			
9	Griffin / Johnson (7) / Fernandez (8F)	6 / PH / 6		SAC 34	—				FC			
		R		1					2			
		H		1	1	1	1		1	2		
		LB		2	1		2	1				

				IP
	Leal			7+
	Gott (8)			2

153

The O's got the run back and another in the fifth on a pair of doubles and a single, and thus matters remained until the eighth, when they turned sticky. Leal allowed singles to Ripken and Murray, and Bobby Cox hooked him and sent out Jim Gott, who promptly filled the sacks by walking the first batter he faced. But not to worry. Gott whiffed Ford, retired Gary Roenicke on a pop foul, and worked Rick Dauer for an inning-ending bouncer to Griffin. Gott did not, it seemed, want to make it seem *too* easy; he stayed behind in the count to each batter he faced, nudging the crowd toward their wits' end.

The frame's bottom and the top of the ninth were uneventful, and the match came down to the Jays' last ups with the home side a run in the hole. Rick Leach led off with a single, putting the tying run aboard. Now up was George Bell. Davis issued a pitch, and Bell roped it on a sudden line past the rightfield fence. Young Davis understood what had happened when the ball was barely off Bell's bat; he slumped to a low crouch and stared at the ground. It was only the fourth homer off him all season – he allows the lowest ratio of h.r.'s in the majors. The crowd, stunned, did not cheer right away. But by the time Bell reached home, 41,000 people were hollering and whistling and banging their seats, and they did not stop until the teams had left the field and Bell had returned for a thunderous curtain call.

It seemed the Jays might win game three of the set at a walk. Oriole starter Scott McGregor did not have his best stuff – his specialties are junk low on the corners and a rainbow bender. The Jays bunched three hits for a pair of runs in the first and a couple more for another run in the fourth. Dave Stieb, meanwhile, shut the O's down cold. He was in trouble in the fourth, when the O's got runners to second and third with two out, but he quickly terminated the frame by whiffing rookie outfielder Mike Young on three pitches. He then downed the side in the fifth on a mere five pitches – a couple of quick groundouts and an infield pop.

But with two out in the seventh Stieb seemed abruptly to lose touch with the strike zone; he walked Young and Roenicke on eight consecutive balls. Oriole skipper Joe Altobelli dispatched lefty thumper Joe Nolan to bat for Dauer, and 36,000 fans stared in unwilling disbelief; their ace seemed to be coming unstrung before their eyes. But Stieb is Stieb. He eliminated Nolan on called strikes. There had, though, been a real problem. Stieb had developed a blister on his pitching hand, and Nolan was the end of his ball game.

Cox sent out Roy Jackson in the eighth, and Jackson seemed off to a good start when Floyd Rayford topped a grounder to Griffin. But no out. Griffin pegged short, the ball hopped past Upshaw, and Rayford hustled down to second. Jackson kept his composure and fanned Bumbry looking, but Ford and Ripken poked seeing-eye nubbers through the infield – a few inches one way or the other, and both were easy outs – to distribute duckies all around the pond. Up came E. Murray.

The Orioles were, at this point, in fourth place in the A.L. East – their loss in game two had dropped them behind the Red Sox in the standings – and this game, if they lost it, would be their seventh straight defeat by the Jays. It was a moment when the Orioles had to do some damage, take some control of their flagging season – a moment customized for their slugging first-sacker. (It is the A.L.'s habit, on such occasions, to evade Murray as best it can; he leads the league in intentional passes. But when the bags are full, there is nowhere to put him.) Murray slammed his triple, and the game was tied.

Baltimore's next batter was Wayne Gross, a lefty, so Cox replaced Jackson with Jimmy Key. Altobelli countered by pinch-hitting Benny Ayala, and Key retired him on a tough grounder on which Garth Iorg made a good play. Counting Rayford's bouncer to Griffin, this was the frame's third out; but because of the miscue, it wasn't. Young batted next – kid against kid – and took two balls. He deposited Key's third

			1	2	3	4	5	6	7	8	9	10	R	H	E	LB
ORIOLES			0	0	0	0	0	0	0	5	0		5	9	0	7
JAYS			2	0	0	1	0	0	0	1	0		4	10	2	8

Orioles

#	Batter	Pos	1	2	3	4	5	6	7	8	9	10
1	Bumbry / Shelby (9F)	8 / 8	X		43			X / −		X	7	
2	Ford	DH	9			8		DP 463		4 −	−	
3	Ripken	6	5L!			K		63		4 −	7D	
4	Murray	3		63		· / −			8D	≡! / 6		
5	Gross / Ayala(8) / Cruz(8F)	5 / PH / 5		K		=			43	5!3		
6	Young	9		−		K!			· / W	⊟		
7	Roenicke	7		8			53		W	8		
8	Dauer / Nolan(7) / Sakata(7F)	4 / PH / 4			63		63		X!		43	
9	Rayford	2			K		4		· E6 / 4	· E5		
	R									5		
	H			1		2		1		4	1	
	LB			1		2			2		2	

IP

Pitcher	IP
McGregor	7 1/3
Stewart (8)	+
T. Martinez (8)	1 2/3

Jays

#	Batter	Pos	1	2	3	4	5	6	7	8	9	10
1	Garcia	4	· = / 4	8		7 / −			K	8		
2	Moseby	8	3F	2F		43			K	X		
3	Bell	7	43		63		7		8	53		
4	Johnson	DH	5 −			· / −	K		7 W			
5	Barfield	9	7 =			7		W		K		
6	Upshaw	3	43		43		7		· =			
7	Iorg / Mulliniks(8) / Fernandez(8)	5 / PH / PR		8		7		9		−		
8	Martinez / Aikens/Collins(8) / Whitt(9F)	2 / PH / 2		· / −		= / 1		7	K!			
9	Griffin	6		−		53		8		9		
	R		2			1				1		
	H		3	2	1	2				2		
	LB		1	2	1	1	1			2		

IP

Pitcher	IP
Stieb	7
Jackson (8)	1
Key (8)	2
Lamp (9)	1

156

offering at roughly the same point beyond the rightfield fence that Bell's h.r. had gone in game two. Roenicke finally popped up to get the Jays off the field, but the damage was done, a two-run Oriole lead. The Jays tried to battle back. A walk and a double forced Altobelli to his pen, and Mulliniks drove a run home with a handy single. But Tippy Martinez then cut Collins down on flailing strikes and retired Griffin to end the threat. The Jays died in the ninth, and the O's had finally won one.

Game four featured more fine pitching, complete games by Jim Clancy and Mike Boddicker. Clancy made only two serious mistakes, a couple of hanging sliders in the top of the second. Roenicke smacked one of them down the left-field line for a double, and Lenn Sakata drove the other into the leftfield bleachers. Clancy did, subsequently, pitch himself into a few jams, but he got away from each unharmed, twice on his own good work – baffling Ripken, Murray, and Gross with two aboard in the third; whiffing Roenicke on called strikes with two aboard in the sixth – and once on the defensive eye-popper of the set. With two out and Bumbry on first in the seventh, Nolan whacked a liner into the rightfield corner, usually a double but not this time. Bell got to the ball quickly and gobbled it up, and Bumbry, heading toward third, thought the better of it and retreated toward second where he was cut down on a flat humming peg from Bell to Griffin. End of inning.

But Clancy's sound work did not much matter. The Jays did notch a run in the third on a double by Mulliniks and a pair of rightside groundouts, but Boddicker was otherwise out of reach – Mulliniks' was the only hit he allowed in the game. Boddicker did falter in the seventh. He hit Dave Collins on the foot with a low curve, and Collins made his way to third on Boddicker's errant pickoff attempts. But he escaped unscathed as Collins was l.o.b. In the final two innings the Jays were six up, six down. Boddicker is another Oriole youngster currently lodged among the league's best starters. His stuff seems to come in three speeds, slow,

			1	2	3	4	5	6	7	8	9	10	R	H	E	LB
ORIOLES			0	2	0	0	0	0	0	0	0		2	7	2	6
JAYS			0	0	1	0	0	0	0	0	0		1	1	0	2

			1	2	3	4	5	6	7	8	9	10
1	Bumbry / Shelby (9F)	8 / 8	x46 —		·· —	K		x96! —			
2	Nolan	DH	3F!		· ω	9		—			
3	Ripken	6	FC		8		53	8D!			
4	Murray	3	6	43			· ω	43			
5	Gross / Cruz (9F)	5 / 5		2F	3		K	⅄			
6	Young	9		K	7		—		K		
7	Roenicke	7		⑧·	K	K!		⅄			
8	Sakata	4		Ⓔ	8		63	9			
9	Dempsey	2		43		63	3F				
		R		2								
		H	1	2	1		1	2				
		LB	1		2		2	1				

IP: Boddicker 9

			1	2	3	4	5	6	7	8	9	10
1	Garcia	4	7		7		63		31		
2	Collins	7	43		43		E1 E1 H		8		
3	Moseby	8	7		8		⅄	43			
4	Upshaw	3		⅄	9!		63				
5	Aikens / Leach (7)	DH / PR		43		K		ω			
6	Bell	9		K		7	7				
7	Mulliniks	5		·= ⑨	31		43				
8	Whitt	2		43		K	8!				
9	Griffin / Johnson (8) / Fernandez (9F)	6 / PH / 6		43		13	K				
		R		1								
		H		1								
		LB					2					

IP: Clancy 9

158

slower, and slowest – mushy garbage. He seems a one-man re-creation of the deadball era.

And so the set ended, a dead heat and worthwhile and instructive stops on the search for the perfect ball game. For the season the Jays were nine-and-four against their feathered Maryland rivals. The years of Oriole dominance of the Jays were ended.

August 17

The search for the perfect game also yields a measure of appallingly bad baseball. With Baltimore's departure, the Jays journeyed to Cleveland for a strange brew of five games with the cellar-dwelling Tribe.

The Jays swept the first two, a twin-bill, with an 8-1 laugher in the opener (win no. eleven for Doyle Alexander) and a 9-5 rout in the nightcap. In the second game the Jays fought back from a 5-0 handicap – Bryan Clark started and was tattooed – on homers by Moseby, Bell, and Garcia; and Lamp came out of the bullpen doghouse for three frames of solid relief and the win. In Detroit, meanwhile, the Tigers dropped a pair to the Angels, so the Jays moved up to only seven and a half games out – roughly where they stood on the same date in May and in June and in July. Hope dawned again. The Jays, it seemed (once more), might make a race of this year's A.L. East after all.

The euphoria lasted less than a day. In game one of a second twin-bill, the following evening, Luis Leal was badly blown out for the first time this season. He allowed ten earned runs in five-plus innings and watched his e.r.a. soar from 3.11 to 3.51. Jimmy Key was then whacked around for a frame – three more Cleveland counters – at which point Bobby Cox, his pen diminished by the pressure of the schedule and a temporary but prohibitive injury to Roy Jackson the night before, sent outfielder Rick Leach to the hillock for his major league pitching debut. Leach allowed three more Indian runs. The Jay offence, meanwhile, was putty in the hamhock paws of rookie hurler Don Schulze, and the final count, 16-1, superceded the June 3 debacle against the Yanks as the Jays' worst drubbing of the season.

Cox's pinchfistedness with his firemen in the opener turned out to be a foresighted move. After four frames of the nightcap, starter Jim Acker was forced to the bench and onto the fifteen-day disabled list by tendinitis in his pitching shoulder. The Jays were left with five innings to play and but a single fresh arm, Jim Gott, in the pen. This ought to have been enough; Gott worked the five innings soundly. But the game was at that point tied 2-2, and so the fledgling reliever's night was not over. The Jays got a run in the top of the tenth, but in the frame's bottom, with two out, a jot from a victory, Gott allowed a single, then walked the bases full. Cox hooked Gott for Key, who walked the tying run home before he notched the third out. Cleveland eventually beat Key in the thirteenth by bunching three singles for a run. *Aha!*, one may say. *The damn bullpen again.* No.

The main story of the game was not the trials of the Jay mound staff, but of the offence, which, in hapless futility, placed seventeen runners aboard with safeties and another six with walks, yet tallied a meagre three counters and accumulated *twenty* l.o.b.'s. This astonishing impotence nearly tied the modern A.L. record for runners left aboard in a thirteen-frame game – twenty-two, by the Boston Red Sox vs. the St. Louis Browns, 8/22/51. And had the game ended an inning earlier, the Jays would have established a new major league mark, either circuit, for l.o.b.'s in a twelve-frame game.

The set-match, next night, was the Jays' through eight and a half. The offence enjoyed a more efficient outing and notched five runs on ten hits. Dave Stieb, working with infinite care, trying to avoid a recurrence of the blister that had forced him from the game in his last start, held Cleveland to two. But after eight the blister rose again, sending Cox to the pen. Dennis Lamp, who had pitched so well only two nights earlier, came out for the ninth and, *wham*, *crack*, *bam* and *smack*, surrendered four hasty runs. Lord, it happened quickly. There went the game. *Aha!*, one may say.

The damn bullpen again. And this time one would be right.

So ended a disheartening set of games. The Tigers, meanwhile, won two more, edging the Jays back to ten games behind.

The Jays have called righty reliever Ron Musselman up from Syracuse to take Acker's place in the pen. Musselman, twenty-nine, has been in the Toronto organization only since June, when he came over from a Texas farm club. Prior to Texas, in 1982, he pitched sixteen passable innings for Seattle, his only major league work. He was apparently the best that Syracuse had to offer at the moment.

Item:

• George Bell is out of his slump and hitting the ball hard again; when Bell is seeing the ball, no Jay hits it harder. (One of the idle amusements at Jay games is watching the fieldside fans frantically scatter when the young batsman lashes a line-drive foul into the stands.) Bell has taken the club lead in h.r.'s and appears on his way toward a new club mark for doubles in a season.* In each of the past two summers, a young Jay has emerged to startle the league – Damaso Garcia in 1982, Lloyd Moseby last year. This season's eye-catcher is Bell. His style of ball is a jubilant aggressiveness which, were his gambles less often successful, might be labelled foolhardiness. But time and again he defies the odds and lands on his feet.

September 3

The Jays are suddenly hot again, closing out August and their season's competition with the A.L. West with eleven wins and five losses. The final calculations:

• Through August the Jays played at a .600 clip, a cheerful stat.; August, the past couple of seasons, has been their undoing. In 1982 and 1983, the years of their emer-

---

* He got there. His thirty-nine two-baggers eclipsed Rick Bosetti's 1979 mark of thirty-five and ranked Bell third in the A.L.

gence from the expansion club morass, they played .555 ball in July and .596 ball in September, but only .418 ball between. This season's record is, however, consistent with the past two years insofar as the Jays' opponents those Augusts were mainly tougher East Division clubs. Their August schedule this year, with fifteen games vs. West Division clubs, against whom they have always played better ball, was softer. From here on out they play only within the East Division; and so September may be their difficult month this season.

• The Jays concluded play against the A.L. West with their strongest record yet against that division:

Jays' Record vs. West Division Clubs, 1982–84

	W	L	PCT.
1982	45	39	.536
1983	50	34	.595
1984	52	32	.619

And they played well against the West on the road this year:

Jays' Home and Away vs. West Division Clubs, 1984

HOME			AWAY		
W	L	PCT.	W	L	PCT.
27	15	.643	25	17	.595

This has helped undo some of the damage done by their .370 record – ten and seventeen – on the road to date against East Division clubs. The Jays played particularly good ball against the Minnesota Twins, allowing the West Division's current frontrunners only a single win in a dozen contests. If the Twins fail in their quest for a playoff berth this year,* they may particularly thank the Jays, who have cleaned their clock, for the shortfall.

Jays vs. West Division Clubs, 1984

VS.	W	L
Minnesota	11	1
Chicago	8	4
Oakland	8	4
Kansas City	7	5
Seattle	7	5
Texas	6	6
California	5	7

The ingredients of the Jays' recent spate of wins are familiar. Sound starting pitching, for one. Each of the Jays' five starters has recorded at least a pair of good starts in the past fortnight. The fifth starter lately has been Dennis Lamp, who seems to have swapped spots with Jim Gott. In each of his first two Jay starts Lamp logged a win. The mound staff's anchor, as usual, has been Dave Stieb, who recovered from his blisterous misadventures earlier this month to pitch three complete games in which he allowed four earned runs. This arithmetic has moved Stieb into the league's e.r.a. leadership, and when he again falls short of the A.L.'s Cy Young award this year, as he likely will, it will be partly because of bad breaks like the blister and partly because of the ineffectiveness of the Jay offence in his games. (His two All-Star Game starts attest to his status in the league.) His offence again failed him against Cleveland August 21. He held the Tribe to one run for eight frames, but the Jays were barely able to notch one. In the ninth Cleveland

* They did.

logged two and the match, the fourth time this season Stieb has been collared with a loss when the Jays scored one or no runs.

But for most of the stretch vs. the West offence was not a problem. Nor was the bullpen, which, in sixteen games, failed only once – in the only game of the season in which the Twins bested the Jays, Dennis Lamp walked home the winning run in the twelfth; it was a couple of days later that he moved into the starting rotation. The pen collected four saves and a couple of wins during the span and allowed only seven earned runs in thirty-seven frames' work for a collective pen e.r.a. of 1.80, A-Okay. (The other three losses, besides Stieb's and Lamp's, were the consequence of bombings of starters. Leal, Clancy, and Alexander each had a downside outing to go with his brace of good starts.) Jimmy Key, in particular, is pitching strongly of late. After some weeks of trouble with the strike zone, he has found his location again. The problem appears to have been mechanical, solved by some tinkering with Key's motion by pitching coach Al Widmar. The pleasant surprise in the pen has been Ron Musselman, who has allowed one earned run in eight i.p.'s and has looked stronger each outing in three middle relief appearances.

The Jays remain in the habit of often doing their damage late, as the line scores of five of the eleven games won illustrate:

Aug. 17	Toronto	0 1 0	0 0 1	0 1 1	— 4	
	Chicago	0 2 0	0 0 0	1 0 0	— 3	
Aug. 19	Toronto	0 0 3	0 0 0	0 0 4	— 7	
	Chicago	0 1 0	0 0 0	3 0 0	— 4	
Aug. 24	Toronto	0 0 0	1 0 0	1 3 1	— 6	
	Minnesota	1 0 0	0 1 0	0 0 0	— 2	
Aug. 28	Chicago	0 3 0	2 0 0	1 0 0	0 0	— 6
	Toronto	1 0 0	0 0 2	3 0 0	0 1	— 7
Aug. 30	Toronto	1 0 0	0 0 0	0 0 3	— 4	
	Chicago	0 1 1	0 0 1	0 0 0	— 3	

164

Eighteen of twenty-eight Jay runs in these matches were put across in the seventh inning or later. But this kind of pattern is not a source for concern – just the opposite. The club is again demonstrating, as it did in its hot streak in May, that, one way or another, it can get the job done; at times it must be done in the final frames.

Coda: You've got to throw the ball over the goddamn plate and give the other man his chance.

Tom Seaver is a White Sock this season because Dennis Lamp is a Blue Jay. When the Jays signed Lamp, an 'A'-type free agent, the Sox plucked Seaver from the 'A'-type compensation pool, where he had been left unprotected by the New York Mets. The loss of Seaver, a sure Hall of Famer and the ace of the legendary 1969 Mets, touched off an 'A'-type brouhaha in Gotham. Tom Terrific, who had returned to New York in 1983 after a five-year stint in Cincinnati red, has an almost mythic stature among New York ball fans.

The Met front office defended its move, saying given its druthers it preferred to lose Seaver than one of the young arms in which the club's future is invested. This explanation did not cut a lot of ice in New York at the time. The young arms were just a bunch of guys named Joe, and the tarring, feathering, and public lynching of the Met suits seemed a distinct possibility. In the intervening months, however, the young Met arms have chewed up the senior circuit and lodged their club firmly in second place in the N.L. East, a better season's outcome than even the most partisan Met fans dared hope for. And if Tom Seaver is not forgotten in New York, his memory has certainly dimmed.

Thus did Tom Seaver shift his quest for 300 career wins to the American League. On August 30 he was working on number 286 and was a bare out away when his plans were shattered by one L. Moseby.

The game ought not have come down to the ninth frame

at all. Jim Clancy had a horrible night during which he allowed seven Sox safeties and a career-high nine walks. But the Sox somehow managed to squander this largess into a mere three runs, and so what might have been a runaway was more nearly a squeaker. Seaver entered the final inning protecting a slim 3-1 lead.

But Seaver has built one of baseball's fine recent pitching careers by prevailing in low-scoring matches. His best years, after all, were with the Mets, rarely an offensive powerhouse. And he did seem, on this night, to have the Jays' number. He had allowed some hits early but, coming into the ninth, had retired ten straight batters with apparent ease. He ran the string to eleven by dispatching Rance Mulliniks. But Willie Upshaw then singled, George Bell beat out an infield nubber, and Willie Aikens drove a run home with a wrong-field single. Score, 3-2. Rick Leach ran for Aikens, and he and Bell advanced to second and third when Ernie Whitt smacked a right-side grounder. Two out. The next scheduled batter was Jesse Barfield, subbing in centre for Lloyd Moseby, whom Bobby Cox gave the night off.

The night before, in a game the Jays lost, in which they left nine runners on base, Moseby had twice had a chance to do damage and had failed both times. He had seemed to be swinging too thoughtlessly for the fences, trying to right matters with one stroke, and by the time he had settled down and tried simply to make contact he had been way behind on the counts and was dead meat. Tonight Cox was resting him.

Barfield, however, had been unable thus far to solve Seaver. The logical choice to pinch hit was Moseby, and Cox sent him out.

Again, the crafty old pro was matched against the young star, and, again, one might have expected the old pro to get the best of the outing. Sox manager Tony LaRussa quickly visited the mound to make sure Seaver did not want relief; Seaver said he did not. With first base open, Moseby expected Seaver might pitch through him to get to Alfredo Griffin, and he took two pitches. The first was a ball, but the second was a humming strike. Moseby knew now Seaver was coming after him. Moseby swung on the next pitch and fouled it away, took a second ball, then fouled three more away.

Moseby stepped out of the batter's box, did a deep knee-bend, and picked up a handful of dirt, which he rubbed in his palms. Seaver was giving him nothing, throwing sucker pitches – stuff that looks fat until you try to hit it. Moseby threw away the dirt and stepped back in the box and fouled off a fifth pitch. Seaver's ninth pitch was a good one, a sneaky wrinkler, and Moseby swung with a mind to foul it off too. But the ball stayed fair, a chip shot that dropped in shallow leftfield behind third base. Bell scored. Leach scored. The Sox were a run down. Cox batted Cliff Johnson for Griffin, and Seaver got him; but the damage was done.

In the frame's bottom, Cox sent out Jimmy Key to pitch to lefty Mike Squires. Key was relieving Jim Gott who had pitched one and a third flawless innings in Clancy's stead. LaRussa went to his bench for a righty pinch-hitter, Greg Luzinski, the Bull; the night before, Luzinski had tagged a homer. Key's first pitch was a ball low and outside, his second a called strike, and Luzinski foul-tipped the third. Key now hooked a curve across the inside corner of the plate at which Luzinski blinked perplexedly. One out. The next batter was more heavy lumber, Ron Kittle, and Key's first offering to Kittle was another called strike. Kittle took a ball, fouled a pitch back, and took another ball. Key walked down behind the mound for a moment's contemplation, returned to the rubber, and threw a pitch way inside. Three-and-two. Key's next pitch was a good low strike. Kittle swung and missed. Two out. Next up was light-hitting shortstop Scott Fletcher, who took a ball, then drove a liner to Tony Fernandez at short. Game done. Seaver will have to wait for another shot at win number 286. The Jays did not let him have it this night.

Items:

• The Jays have brought up five players from Syracuse, where the season is over, to help with the stretch drive: Kelly Gruber, Toby Hernandez, Mitch Webster, Fred Manrique, and Ron Shepherd.

• The Tigers have played a stretch of .500 ball of late, and so the Jays have closed Detroit's lead to eight and a half games.

Standings, A.L. East, Sept. 3

	W	L	PCT.	GB
Detroit	88	49	.642	—
Toronto	79	57	.581	8½
Baltimore	73	62	.541	14
New York	72	63	.533	15
Boston	72	64	.529	15½
Cleveland	61	77	.442	27½
Milwaukee	56	80	.412	31½

TWELVE

Cat on a Greased Pole

Sutters and Gossages don't grow on trees.
— Tony Kubek

All we can do is keep playing and see what happens.
— Bobby Cox

September 6

The days are shorter now, nights nippy, kids back in school. Summer and baseball are nearly done. No box scores soon, no radio games, no noise in the bleachers. But first there is serious business to do.

The Jays have begun two weeks that matter, seven games with New York and six with Detroit. The Yanks were trouble for the Jays in June, four of six matches lost and a fifth a near thing, and they have played the best ball in the league since the All-Star break:

Standings, A.L. East, Since All-Star Break

	W	L	PCT.	GB
New York	36	17	.679	—
Boston	31	21	.596	4½
Detroit	31	22	.585	5
Toronto	29	23	.558	6½
Baltimore	27	23	.540	7½
Cleveland	28	28	.500	9½
Milwaukee	17	33	.340	17½

And the Tigers have been trouble for everyone. The Jays must whip both to keep alive their dimming pennant chances.

They got off to a bad start. Playing in New York, they dropped two of three – close, well-played matches but two more nails in the coffin.

They were shut out in game one by a young Yank hurler named Joe Cowley, only the third time this season the Jays have been goose-egged. Luis Leal pitched well, too, but allowed a scratch run in the seventh and a homer by Dave Winfield in the eighth, and that was that.

The Jays struck early for three in game two, and Jim Clancy pitched good ball through six. But the Yanks then pulled ahead on one nibbled run and three more on another homer by Winfield. Winfield's b.a. against the Jays this year is .462. In this at-bat Clancy got ahead of him oh-two but could not rub him out. Winfield took three balls and tagged Clancy's full count offering over the leftfield fence.

Still, the Jays were not out of it. They clawed three runs in the eighth on a pair of singles, a pair of walks, a pair of stolen bases, a sac. fly, and a wild pitch – exploitative baseball. With two down in the inning's bottom, Don Mattingly doubled, returning Winfield to the plate, but this time Roy Jackson fanned him swinging. Jimmy Key pitched the ninth and logged his season's eighth save, and the Jays had finally won their first game at Yankee Stadium this year. There was, though, bad news, too. Lloyd Moseby, jerking away from a pitch way inside – he seemed to do an abrupt deep limbo – strained a ligament in his right knee, and will be lost for a game or longer.

The Jays had to play catch-up again in game three. The Yanks eked out two early, and it wasn't until the sixth that the Jays finally got on the board – a walk, a single, and a two-out triple by Mitch Webster, subbing for Moseby in centre. Alfredo Griffin then bagged the go-ahead run with a reprise of the same play he had used to beat K.C. in an extra-inning game in May, a bunt dragged up the first-base line which he beat out by a sliver of a second as Webster scored from third. The Yanks nearly tied matters in the inning's bottom when Dave Winfield smacked one to deep left. It cleared the fence by about a foot, where it landed in a leaping George Bell's upstretched glove. It was Bell's first defensive delight of the match; he timed the ball perfectly and literally stole back a run.

The Yanks did the score in the seventh on a couple of hits, and the game was not finally resolved until the bottom of the tenth. Roy Jackson got one out when George Bell made a shoestring catch of a tailing liner by Mattingly, his second gem of the night. It was a good thing that, once committed and running full-tilt, he made the play, or the ball would have gone to the wall for an inside-the-park homer. Winfield popped to centre for a second out, but Yank d.h. Don Baylor then worked Jackson to a three-and-one count and rode an inside fastball into the leftfield stands.

While the Jays were in New York, the Orioles were in Detroit taking two of three from the Tigers. After the second game of the Yankee set, the match they won, the Jays had edged to just seven and a half back of Detroit. But in the end nothing changed; they stayed eight and a half back. Tomorrow the Tigers came to Toronto for three, a set the Jays must sweep.

September 10
So much for the old pennant race.

The Jay-Detroit set was a sweep all right. Trouble is, wrong team swept. Imagine a tiger with bits of blue feather stuck in the fur around his jaws. The Tigers' line in the clubhouse was, hell, we're just playing this thing one game at a time, we've got a nice lead, no big deal. But on the field they came at the Jays ruthlessly, as though every pitch, every out, every extra base might decide matters. They meant, it seemed, to make it clear to the Jays that first place in the A.L. East is a settled issue, that the Jays had best turn their energies simply to hanging onto second.

More clues to the Tiger puzzle: strength up the middle (Parrish, Whitaker and Trammell, Lemon); infield play which is nearly flawless, especially on the right side, where Whitaker and Bergman are almost impermeable; pitchers who consistently stay ahead of the count, forcing opposition hitters onto the defensive and walking few (in these games, only five); batters who whack clutch hits as a matter of course, most notably homers (they knocked seven h.r.'s in these games, each at a moment which counted – no vanity homers here); a bench deep with players who can come in and do the job (pinch-hit, provide late-inning defence, sub for a regular). They are an awfully good ballteam.

Yet they are not *that* much better than the Jays. The Jays hit and field skilfully, too. The Jays' starting staff is among the best in the majors. The Jays are also capable of clutch heroics. Oh, the Tigers have the edge, no doubt about that now, but it is not so much an edge in talent as in seasoning, instinct, savvy. They are a hungrier club than the Jays and seem to know better how to go about the business of winning. One constantly recalls their cold-blooded dominance this season of other clubs' home turf and, too, the frequent lessons that some of these young Jays are not yet in full command of their gifts. But the Tigers are not *that* much better, not by any measure but one: their pen. And in their games in Toronto the Tigers found the Jays' soft belly and mauled it.

In game one the Jays tallied four runs early. Two were scratched, for which the catalyst was Alfredo Griffin. He drove a runner home from first with a modest sac. bunt on which the Tigers seemed momentarily hapless and committed two errors, putting Griffin on third. He then scored an at-bat later on a routine grounder on which he had no business scoring. The other two were on a h.r. by Willie Aikens (*crack* and gone). Doyle Alexander shut Detroit down through seven.

But with two on and two out in the eighth, Kirk Gibson took Alexander downtown to pull the Tigers within one, 4-3. Alexander then walked Lance Parrish, and that was his night. Jimmy Key came in and pitched to only one batter, Barbaro Garbey, who dropped a soft two-strike bloop just past the mound on which the Jay infield could not make a play. Base-hit. Key could be faulted here for nothing but lucklessness. Roy Jackson now came in and committed a nightmare, walking the bases full on four pitches, then walking the tying run home. Jim Gott finally got the third out. In the ninth and tenth, after Gott, Bobby Cox went to Bryan Clark and Ron Musselman, trying, somehow, to manufacture a stopper out of the Jay relief corps. He failed.

The game's decisive blow was a three-run homer banged by Dave Bergman off Musselman in the top of the tenth. Bergman had also knocked a tenth-inning three-run homer to resolve an earlier Jay-Tiger match this year. He seems to enjoy Jay relief pitching.

And where were the Jays while all this Detroit scoring was occurring? Stymied, by the Tiger pen. Bill Scherrer whiffed Ernie Whitt with two aboard in the sixth. Doug Bair faced four batters and recorded four economical outs (K, 4-3, 4-3, 4-3) in the sixth and seventh. Willie Hernandez stopped the Jays cold through the eighth, ninth, and tenth.

A few words about Hernandez. He entered the Jay set with an e.r.a. of 1.98 in 123 innings' work. He had come into twenty-eight games that were save situations and earned saves in all twenty-eight. He had won ten games and lost two, and the losses had occurred in matches which were tied when he entered – i.e., not once this season had he blown a Tiger lead. Of thirty-one runners aboard when he came to the mound, only nine had scored, and three had tallied on Tiger E.'s and a fourth on a Tiger d.p. This is mighty fine relief work. Willie Hernandez has, in the end, been the biggest difference between the Tigers and Jays this season.

Hernandez has wildly exceeded Detroit's notion of his role when they acquired him this spring. His stats in seven prior major league seasons had been journeyman stuff: thirty-four wins, thirty-two losses, twenty-seven saves, a 3.72 e.r.a., mostly in the service of the Chicago Cubs, for the latter part of last season with the Phils. Detroit had been looking only for a competent southpaw to take some pressure off their pen's other ace, Aurelio Lopez, who nearly burned himself out last season. But Hernandez seems to have been incontent with simply journeyman status. Besides a basic major league repertoire, he has a cut-fastball, learned from Ferguson Jenkins when both were Cubs, and a screwball, learned from Mike Cuellar in Puerto Rico one winter. And he has the icy nerve relief work requires. His blossoming this year has been one of the A.L.'s pleasures.*

There was a lot of nitpicking one might have done after the game. Cox might have pinch-hit for Whitt against southpaw Scherrer. Because he platoons, Whitt rarely faces lefties; he does, however, often pound Detroit pitching. Cox might have gone to Key two batters sooner, to face Gibson, who bats left and who tagged the eighth-frame homer; but Cox, not without reason, has lately seemed timid about reaching into his pen. Had Ernie Whitt managed to hang onto a two-strike foul tip off Garbey's bat in the eighth – the pitch immediately before the one Garbey looped past Key – the Jays would have come out of the inning still a run ahead. But this is all just a smokescreen. The nub of the issue is that the Tiger pen was effective, the Jay pen was not, and that was the story not just of this game but has been the story of a lot of the season.**

In the second game Detroit led 4-2 when the Jay firecrew broke out its gas cans. Bryan Clark, working in the top of the eighth in relief of Luis Leal, got in trouble, and Dennis Lamp entered the game and dittoed Jackson's nightmare of the first match. With two aboard, he walked the sacks full, then walked a run home. Lamp's frustration and anger with himself showed in his face as his pitches kept missing the plate. It wasn't supposed to *be* this way. After a pair of Jay errors, four more Tigers scored. The Jays, meanwhile, after knocking out the Tabs' starter, were quelled by Scherrer

* He was baseball's player of the year. At season's end he won the A.L.'s Cy Young and MVP awards.
** Late in the summer an Ontario Hydro ad turned up on TV which featured a succession of Jay relievers getting racked, hooked, and routed for the showers where, in spite of their sudden numbers, they find an ample sufficiency of electrically heated hot water. They shower in steamy, gloomy melancholy.

and Lopez. Lopez, working in tandem with Hernandez this season, has thus far logged ten wins, no losses, and thirteen saves.

In game three Detroit again led 4-2 and had two runners aboard – it was the top of the seventh – when Cox sent out Bryan Clark to face Gibson. Gibson rode Clark's very first pitch deep, *deep* past the fence in right-centre. Parrish doubled, Darrell Evans walked, and Cox hooked Clark for Jim Gott. Gott did not allow another Detroit base runner for the match's duration, but it was too late to matter. While Gott was working, Scherrer and Hernandez were working, too, and they allowed the Jays squat.

The Jays might have lost the games anyway, even apart from their pen's misdeeds – in games two and three the Tigers were already leading when the Jay relievers clocked in. But the games still might have been satisfying, if ultimately more heartbreaking, baseball. Instead, they were maulings. Instead of coming into the final frames of the second and third games trailing by just a couple, the Jays came in deep in the hole, which is entirely different.

The set was more than just three games lost. For the Jays and their fans, it was an ugly, gloomy weekend. Until now there had been a chance, just a chance, the miracle might happen. No longer. The Jays are still not mathematically out of it. If Detroit loses nearly all their games from here on out and the Jays win nearly all of theirs . . . mm. The Jays' pennant race is ended for this year.

The season, however, is not ended. After these losses, even second place is no sure thing for the Jays. The Orioles are now only two and a half games back. The Yanks, with whom the Jays still play four, are three and a half back. The Red Sox, with whom the Jays play six, are five back. Any one of these clubs can pull its season from the fire by dislodging the Jays from the Tigers' tail, and they have all lately played winning ball. The schedule has three weeks remaining, twenty games, and the Jays will be fighting in the trenches every inch of the way.

Items:

- Moseby's knee is healing but was too fragile for him to play in the Tiger set. Without him the Jays still had a pretty good outfield – Barfield in centre, Bell in right, Collins in left – but there is no doubt Moseby's absence hurt. For all that, good clubs are still good clubs even with stars on the bench. Detroit, for example, has lost Jack Morris, Alan Trammell, and Chet Lemon, at one time or another, to injury this season. Moseby will return to the lineup this week.

- There is suddenly a lot of talk about solving the Jays' pen problem by converting Dave Stieb to relief work next year. It is a measure of how critical the stopper's role has become that there is serious musing about converting one of the league's best starters to a fireman. The idea is either harebrained or brilliant. It is not entirely unprecedented. The Yanks, for example, without Rick Gossage this year, dispatched southpaw Dave Righetti to the pen, where he has done good work. The Yanks would not have enjoyed their mid-summer surge without him. But while Righetti was not without gifts as a starter – last season he threw a no-hitter – he was by no measure in Stieb's class.

September 14

The Tiger has had its kill; and now the race is among the jackals for the leavings. And if it does not matter much in the long course of baseball history who wins the race – no one will ask, forty years hence, who was runnerup to the Tigers in the A.L. East in 1984 – it matters a lot to the jackals. It matters especially to the Jays. After lodging in second place nearly all season, they do not want to collapse in the schedule's final days. "If we drop out of second," Buck Martinez said this week, "it will be like kicking five months of hard work down the drain."

In their first match after the Tigers' departure, again against the Yanks, Dave Stieb was not sharp, and the Jays played flatfooted ball. They logged their fifth loss in a row. But on the following night they turned it around with a 10-3 rout. How their scoring started, before the game became a laugher, is noteworthy. Their first rally began with a nifty base-hit bunt laid down by, of all people, Cliff Johnson. Johnson seemed to be trying to demonstrate a lesson to the young Jay swatters: there are times when one forgets the long ball and just tries to get on base, get something started. Upshaw singled, and the key hit of the inning, driving home Johnson and moving Upshaw to third, from which he subsequently scored on a sac. fly, was struck by another Jay vet, Buck Martinez. Martinez' b.a. has been a homely critter this season – currently .220, and it has never gotten much above that. But there are other meaningful measures of batwork. Run production average, for instance, gauges a player's scoring involvement per at-bat. The formula is: runs + r.b.i.'s – h.r.'s ÷ a.b.'s. By this yardstick, after one hundred and forty-four games, Martinez is among the Jays' thumpers:

Jay Run Production Leaders

Moseby	.291
Johnson	.279
Upshaw	.267
Barfield	.254
Martinez	.249
Bell	.243

The Jays split their season's final two games with the Yanks, holding their own against the Bombers in the standings. During the set, Dennis Lamp won his third start of three as a Jay, and it may be that his future in Toronto will be in the rotation rather than the pen – he may be better suited to a role in which he knows, on a given day, whether or not he will be working. And Luis Leal, who has been on hard times lately, seeming to tire as the season winds down, dropped his fourth consecutive start. The Orioles, meanwhile, took two of three from Detroit, winning their season series against the Tigers seven to six*, and the Red Sox dropped two of three to the Brewers. The jackal division at the moment:

Toronto	82	64	.562	—
Baltimore	79	65	.549	2
New York	78	67	.538	3½
Boston	76	69	.524	5½

The Demon Blue Jays' revenge against the Orioles looms large in how the two clubs may finally place in the standings.

September 17

The Jays have journeyed to Detroit, won a game and lost two, as the Tigers illustrated once more why they are the A.L.'s top guns this year. Willie Aikens homered twice in the match the Jays won, the kind of slugging that has been his custom in seasons past. (Aikens will woodshed his batting stroke in Venezuela this winter, hoping to arrive in Florida next spring loaded for bear.) Jim Clancy and Jimmy Key, who continues to pitch well, carefully defused Detroit's bats. Final score, 7-2.

And now a quick quiz: in match two of the set, the Tigers scored just twice, but the Jays managed only one run and logged a bare three safeties. Who, for five marks, was the Jay hurler? Correct, Dave Stieb, again tagged with a loss in a game in which he lowered his league-leading e.r.a. among starters (currently 2.50). The phenomenon at work here may be dubbed the Stieb Effect; and one of the reasons the Jay offence may often have trouble in games Stieb

* The Orioles were one of two clubs who played winning ball against Detroit this year; the other was the Red Sox.

works is that his presence on the mound frequently appears to inspire opposing ballsmen to unaccustomed feats of Jaybashing. The Tiger starter in the game Stieb lost was Milt Wilcox, whose record against the Jays over the past two seasons has been no wins, four losses and an e.r.a. of 7.25. But in this match he held the Jays to one hit, one walk, and one run over seven frames.

The third game of the set was a fizzle, reminiscent of the Jays' early days when a lot of games were in the trashbin before even one inning's play. Bobby Cox had announced Dennis Lamp as his starter but, at the last minute, changed plans and went with Bryan Clark instead. His reasoning was that the Tiger attack seems less volatile against south-paws. Perhaps as a general rule this is true, but the Tabs had no trouble sorting out Clark. After two-thirds of a frame Detroit led 4-0 and the Jay lefty was in the clubhouse. The match's final score was 8-3. So much for bright ideas. And so much, this season, for the Tigers.

The Red Sox, meanwhile, won two of three, and the Orioles and Yanks dropped two of three – standings in the jackal league are a little tighter:

Toronto	83	66	.557	—
Baltimore	80	67	.544	2
New York	79	69	.534	3½
Boston	78	70	.527	4½

Baltimore plays three with New York this week, while the Jays host the Bosox for three, a chance to shake at least one of their pursuers.

September 20
Nothing is clearer.
The Jays' first game with the Sox was sloppily played on

both sides but a see-saw, compulsively tense. A Jay error figured in an early Sox run (1-0), and after the Jays had edged ahead (2-1), a second Jay error figured as the Sox tied it up (2-2). Boston slipped in front when Mike Easler homered in the top of the seventh (3-2), but Boston E.'s now started to reckon in the scoring. The Jays relocked the match in the bottom of the seventh on a solitary hit and a pair of Boston miscues (3-3). The Sox inched ahead again on a single and a double in the top of the ninth (4-3). But the Jays logged two and the game as well in the bottom of the ninth on a couple of walks, a couple of singles, and yet a third Boston error (5-4). Not All-Star ball, but at this point of the season the Jays will take their wins any way they can get them.

The stars of the match were Doyle Alexander and Dave Collins. Alexander, who pitched his eighth complete game, also conducted a tutorial on how to field his position (no glove lapses here), playing impeccable defence and twice choking Boston rallies, once by excising a lead runner on a nice play to third, once by turning a glitzed sac. bunt into a quick double play. Collins sustained the Jays' ninth-inning rally with a grounder to third, which he beat out for a hit; he scored the winning run a moment later.

In the second and third games the Sox logged twenty runs on twenty-four hits, of which eight were homers (two in each match by Dwight Evans). Jay starters Luis Leal and Jim Clancy were blown clean out of the water – the Sox led 10-2 after six innings of game two and 9-1 after five innings of game three. At least one is not reduced to muttering again about the bullpen.

The Jays did not look sharp in either game, have not looked sharp for several days now, and one wonders if they have not shot their bolt, played too hard too futilely (chasing the runaway Tiger) for too long, if they are not running on empty as the season wanes. Since Labour Day they have batted .230, scored fewer than four runs an outing, had a staff e.r.a. of 4.57, and lost eleven of sixteen games. Baseball's long season is often especially hard on young teams because young players have often not learned very well yet how to pace themselves. It is not accidental that among the key players in the Jays' scarce recent wins are the vets – Alexander, Collins, Martinez, Johnson. The marathon, remember, is an old guy's race; it is sprints at which youngsters excel.

The Jays' battering this month at the paws of the Tigers seemed particularly demoralizing for some of the younger Jays. Accepting defeat (which does not mean you like getting beat – getting beat stinks – but it means you do not let it get you too badly down on yourself) is sometimes one of the hardest lessons to learn. And the bulwark of the club, the players who don't platoon – Moseby, Upshaw, Bell, Garcia – have played almost daily since April, a tough row to hoe. But, for all that, the Jays have been streaky all year, and there are still ten games to go.

While the Jays were losing two to the Sox, the Yanks were sweeping three from the Orioles, who have slipped a notch. The jackal division has tightened even further:

Toronto	84	68	.553	—
New York	82	69	.543	1½
Baltimore	80	70	.533	3
Boston	80	71	.530	3½

If the Jays do not come alive their last week, a fifth-place finish is more than just a remote possibility. And they must win five of their last ten matches to equal last year's record of eighty-nine wins. Six of ten will tie them with the 1976 K.C. Royals for the second-best record by an expansion club in its eighth season. Seven of ten will move them past the Royals; but this seems unlikely now.

September 24

The Jays are clinging like a cat to a greased pole. They have split four with the Brewers. At one point the Yanks edged to within a game of them, but the Tigers bludgeoned the Yanks back down a notch to give the Jays a bare safety margin.

The stars of the games the Jays won were once more Collins and Alexander. Collins scored three runs and drove in two more in a 6-4 match which Dave Stieb pitched like a Saturday morning adventure serial, constantly working into impossible jams, then escaping by the skin of his teeth. This knack for extricating himself from horrible peril is the quality most frequently mentioned by those who are touting Stieb for the stopper's role next season. He needed help in the end from Jimmy Key, who closed out the ninth to log a save. Collins, in the game, stole two bases and, at fifty-eight thefts and counting, is fashioning a new club high. (The previous high was Damaso Garcia's fifty-four in 1982.)* In the Jays' second win of the set, a 2-1 squeaker, Alexander pitched a three-hit complete game and Rance Mulliniks twice drove home Moseby for the Jay counters.

Appreciating baseball is an incremental business. Neither Collins' nor Alexander's work in the matches won will be lodged in the record books beside sluggers' four-homer outings or star hurlers' perfect games. What catches the eye here is not the spectacular but rhythmic disciplined craft which, inning by inning, game by game, adds up to excellence. To really ken what Collins and Alexander have meant to this team one must have watched them day after day in all the constant small situations that make up a season. To suggest they may be the Jays' MVP's this year is

---

* The Jays also fashioned a new team high in s.b.'s, a league-leading 193. The league average was ninety-three, and the old Jay club high was last season's 131.

to take nothing away from Lloyd Moseby or Dave Stieb, gifted athletes who have had good seasons; a club gets players like them once a decade. But one knows they will have better seasons. Collins and Alexander, on the other hand, have had the best seasons of their careers, and as one watches them work, one sees years of practice and learning honed to art.

About the games the Jays lost to Milwaukee, the less said, the better. Dennis Lamp endured his first infelicitous start as a Jay as the Brewers racked him in one match for five early runs. Don Sutton, meanwhile, still pitching strongly at thirty-nine, held the Jays in close check and logged career win 280; like Charlie Hough, Sutton is another Dodger gone awandering as he brings a fine career toward a close. In the second loss the Jays twice took the lead; the bullpen twice failed to hold it.

The latter game was the last the Jays will play in Toronto this year and might, under other circumstances, have been occasion for celebration. Instead, it was more occasion for frustration – Garth Iorg smashing his bat against the turf after popping up with the bases loaded, failing to shatter it, and smashing it again; Jesse Barfield punching his fist against the rightfield wall as a Brewer homer sailed over his head, less in anger, it seemed, than desperation; George Bell, infuriated by a called third strike, violently divesting himself of his batting helmet beside the plate and enjoying summary ejection; and the fans, twenty-odd thousand strong, sitting in crestfallen silence as yet another match slipped away to the team with the major leagues' worst record this season. (The Jays are two-and-eight against Milwaukee thus far.) But, in the end, in spite of the loss, there was warm applause. The Jays played .605 ball on home turf this year, their best record here yet, and if the match was a downer, the season was not.

The Jays notched another record at home this year: not a

single rainout. The only game rescheduled was one can-celled because of a freak windstorm in late April. In sea-sons past, the Jays have averaged about three rainouts a year. This is something on which Toronto's domed stadium boosters may want to chew – the people who are deter-mined to give Toronto one of the architectural Fat Alberts named after politicians the world over. The damned thing isn't needed. This is a different argument from that of tradi-tionalists whose case is that baseball is meant to be played outdoors. True, playing baseball indoors is like listening to fine music in an underground parking garage. But this is a separate issue from whether there is cause for building a covered stadium in the first place. Baseball has, in any case, been played outdoors for some time now in Boston and Detroit, cities whose climates are pretty much the same as Toronto's, and seems to have prospered in these places.

So the home season has ended. And meanwhile the Red Sox have swept three from Baltimore. There will be no blistering Oriole stretch drive this year. The jackal league:

Toronto	86	70	.551	—
New York	83	71	.539	2
Boston	83	72	.535	2½
Baltimore	81	73	.526	4

This week's matches feature the Jays in Boston and Yanks in Baltimore. If you forget the Tigers, it's a hell of a race.

September 27
There is something left in the tank after all. Playing in Fen-way, the Jays edged the Bosox two games to one and have pretty well iced second place. The Yanks and Red Sox still have a mathematical chance – the Orioles dropped two of

three to New York this week, and the best they can do now is third – but the combination of circumstance required for the Jays to be headed is unlikely.

In usual Fenway tradition, the Boston games were chock full of scoring, forty-nine runs in all, an average of nearly a run per half-inning. The Red Sox have also maintained the club's tradition of offensive power. The 1984 Sox outfield – Jim Rice, lf; Tony Armas, cf; Dwight Evans, rf – will be only the third in baseball history in which each member has tallied at least one hundred r.b.i.'s. The earlier trios that accomplished this feat were Bobby Veach, lf; Ty Cobb, cf; Harry Heilmann, rf (the 1921 Tigers) and Riggs Stephenson, lf; Hack Wilson, cf; Kiki Cuyler, rf (the 1929 Chicago Cubs). Other traditions this year's Sox have sustained are a dearth of team speed and a mediocre defence, traits that especially show up in Boston's record on artificial turf, where they have been a losing club.

The Jays barely squeaked out game one, 9-8, and were blown out of game two, 14-6, but recovered to win the final match 8-4, in good part on the strength of Doyle Alexander's pitching. The Sox scored all their runs in one chaotic inning; otherwise Alexander deftly milled the Boston lumber to sawdust. The win was his seventeenth, which tied his personal high for wins in a season (seventeen and eleven with Texas in 1977) and tied the Jay season-high for wins by a pitcher (Dave Stieb, twice, 1982 and 1983).

The Boston set was occasion for a godawful injustice done Dave Stieb, which may cost him the year's e.r.a. title. It occurred during the second game and illustrates the power wielded by official scorers. Stieb, for the second time in succession, was not sharp; the length of the season may be getting to him, too. But a dull Dave Stieb is still preferable to most hurlers on an average day, and had the Jay infield handled their chances better, Stieb might have worked himself out of what turned out instead to be a horrible inning.

186

The main culprit was Tony Fernandez, playing short, and one particular chance he booted, a grounder up the middle that caromed off his glove and into the outfield, was officially scored a hit. It was just an ordinary bit of home-field scoring – crediting a local batter with an arguable safety, though in this case the arguability was moot insofar as Fernandez did put his glove on the ball and, had he handled it, would have made the play. Awarding the batter a hit was balderdash. In other circumstances the scorer's decision might have meant little but slight inflation of a Bosock b.a. But in this case, when the inning's arithmetic was done, Stieb ended up with six earned runs, more than he usually surrenders in a couple of games. His e.r.a. ballooned to 2.79, a fraction shy of Baltimore's Mike Boddicker, at 2.78. Stieb and Boddicker each have a start left, and so the numbers may still change in Stieb's favour.

The Jays had, besides Alexander, a number of stars in the Boston set. Both George Bell and Cliff Johnson popped a pair of homers, and Jesse Barfield, Ernie Whitt, and Kelly Gruber also knocked h.r.'s. It was Gruber's first major league hit, and the Fenway crowd, which had earlier been getting on the kid's case, rewarded him with a lengthy round of raucous applause, insisting he return from the dugout for a bow, which, tugged out by Jesse Barfield, he did. Lloyd Moseby hit .461, with a double in each match. And in game one, protecting a one-run lead in the bottom of the ninth, Ron Musselman survived the volcanic heart of the Bosox' order for his first major league save.

But the brightest Jay star of this latest Battle of the Fens was the Iron Man, Alfredo Griffin. No, he notched no homers or extra-base hits or stunning bits of baseball *immortalia*. Subbing at second for Damaso Garcia, out since last weekend with a jammed heel, Griffin just played his game. He tallied five hits, four runs, and a couple of ribbies and squeezed the Boston defence for every conceivable extra base available. His bag here included a run scored when, on third, he virtually forced a young Sox pitcher to commit a balk. And he played solid defence, conceding the Sox nothing in the field. Musselman weathered that final inning of game one only because Griffin, flinging himself headlong, prevented a sharp hopper up the middle from going to the outfield and stopped the tying run from scoring. It seemed anyplace one looked in these games, Griffin was at the heart of the action.

Griffin was not, in Boston, a three-day wonder. He has been one of the Jays who, since Labour Day, particularly since the debacle of the Tiger series in Toronto, has not seemed bedraggled. He has batted .320, had a run production average of .280, and been, for the most part, rock-solid in the field this month. And the contrast of Griffin and Tony Fernandez of late illustrates how the September stretch drive sorts out vets from kids. Fernandez, since Labour Day, is batting .228, has an r.p.a. of .105, and has been occasionally quite shaky in the field. At least a few times he has been excessively timid, laying back on ground balls and managing only one out when a d.p. was in order. At other times he has been excessively exuberant – the ball he slapped into the outfield during Stieb's nightmarish inning in game two had been bound, before he altered its course, into the glove of Griffin, about to make a routine force play at second. This sporadic recent ineptitude is not characteristic of Fernandez's game. The kid has too many skills not to turn out to be a pretty good ballplayer, and his month's work has also included some good batwork and pretty fielding. But for all his gifts, he still needs to learn how to play this game – not just inning by inning or game by game but week by month by season.

Griffin's value to the Jays is partly that, like Collins, he's often a sparkplug, and he sparked this week in Boston, as he has through this whole hard month, when the team most badly needed it. If one imagines a baseball club as a structure built of bricks – Moseby, Upshaw, Bell, Stieb, Clancy – the image also needs mortar to bind the pieces together – players like Griffin. This metaphor will elude sophisticated statistical treatment of the game, but baseball's numbers often conceal as many truths as they reveal.*

There are only three games left now. The record of the 1976 K.C. Royals remains within the Jays' reach.

Standings, A.L. East, Sept. 27

	W	L	PCT.	GB
Detroit	102	56	.646	—
Toronto	88	71	.553	14½
New York	85	73	.538	17
Boston	84	74	.532	18
Baltimore	83	75	.525	19
Cleveland	71	87	.449	31
Milwaukee	65	93	.411	37

* The most noteworthy weakness in Griffin's game is a reluctance to draw bases on balls. He has accepted only four free passes in more than 400 bats this year. This distaste for the walk also seems to affect the Jays' other Dominicans. Damaso Garcia has drawn only sixteen b.b.'s in more than 600 at-bats, and George Bell has managed only twenty-four walks in more than 600 a.b.'s. The Jays have remained through the season well below the league average in drawing walks, and so their on-base percentage remains less than it might be.

THIRTEEN

One for the Mantelpiece

After all those losses, all those hard times, I wanted to be around when the good things started to happen.
— Ernie Whitt

In the country of baseball, time is the air we breathe, and the wind swirls us backward and forward, until we seem so reckoned in time and seasons that all time and all seasons become the same.
— Donald Hall

October 1

The Jays' final set of the season, against the Brewers in Milwaukee, started poorly. Brewer backstop Jim Sundberg defused the Jay offence in the first match by apprehending, *in flagrante delicto*, four Jay base runners attempting theft. In the late frames the Brewer pen did its job, while the Jay pen did not. Final score, Brewers 4-3 in eleven.

The following day, the Jays nearly lost another one-run match as Dave Stieb was mediocre for eight frames and allowed the Brewers four counters, while his offence managed only three. (He failed to regain the league e.r.a. lead, and the title will go to Mike Boddicker.) With two on and two out in the ninth – still, at season's end, the Jays were the Cardiac Kids – Ernie Whitt pinch-singled, Rick Leach pinch-walked, and Fred Manrique, who had come in to pinch-field a frame earlier, singled, too, to draw the Jays ahead by one. Stieb dispatched the Brewers in the inning's bottom, and the Jays had clinched second place.

As one watched the match, a clutch of questions jangled. How will the club solve the middle-infield dilemma? Manrique, who seems ready to step into a utility spot, gives the Jays even more depth at second and short, and either Damaso Garcia or Alfredo Griffin will likely be gone come spring, traded for relief pitching. And what will happen in the outfield, where the Jays now have four everyday players? Lloyd Moseby and George Bell are fixtures, and so the issue comes down to the other two. Collins, besides speed, offers seasoning and savvy, but Jesse Barfield, the odd man out this year, offers power. It seems almost unthinkable to consider trading Collins after all he has meant to the club this year. But Barfield, seven years Collins' junior, must play every day next season – if not in Toronto, elsewhere. And if the Jays are to remain a serious contender in the A.L. East, they need to acquire more power, not lose it. Tricky.

Interlude: a brief thesis about power, the Jays, and the A.L. East.

The Jays did, as anticipated, have a difficult September this year – since September 3 they have played .385 ball – just as in past years they had difficult Augusts, the months of their pennant-stretch matches against East Division clubs. And with their losing record in intradivision play this season, they dropped a couple of notches from last year when, for the first time, they managed a break-even record vs. the East. The numbers:

Jays' Record vs. East Division Clubs, 1982–84

	W	L	PCT.
1982	33	45	.423
1983	39	39	.500
1984	37	41	.474

It was on the road that the Jays had particular trouble against East Division clubs this year:

Jays' Home and Away vs. East Division Clubs, 1984

HOME			AWAY		
W	L	PCT.	W	L	PCT.
22	17	.564	15	24	.385

A reason sometimes offered for the Jays' poor job against the East on the road is playing surface. Away from their artificial turf at home, on the grass fields on which the rest of the division plays, their speed and good fielding matter less, and they are a weaker club. True, some of the difference between their home and road records vs. the East is likely a function of home-field advantage – i.e., playing in a familiar park in front of the home crowd, quite apart from playing surface. But the disparity seems greater than can be accounted for by home-field advantage alone. There is support for this argument in their record against West Division clubs in which the factor of home-field advantage can be isolated:

Jays vs. West Division Clubs, 1984

HOME			ROAD/TURF			ROAD/GRASS		
W	L	PCT.	W	L	PCT.	W	L	PCT.
27	15	.643	11	7	.611	14	10	.583

The Jays appear to have a small but distinct advantage against the West Division on road/turf. And, overall, playing surface appears to be a factor in Jay fortunes.

Still, these stats may be a consequence of one year's idiosyncrasies – e.g., the Jays hammered the Twins this season and were hammered, in turn, by the Brewers. So before one reaches any conclusions, one may want a longer look. Here are the same stats for the past three seasons:

Jays Home and Away vs. East Division Clubs, 1982–84

HOME			AWAY		
W	L	PCT.	W	L	PCT.
63	54	.538	46	71	.393

Jays vs. West Division Clubs, 1982–84

HOME			ROAD/TURF			ROAD/GRASS		
W	L	PCT.	W	L	PCT.	W	L	PCT.
79	47	.627	30	24	.555	38	34	.528

The patterns are just the same. When idiosyncrasies are randomized across three years, playing surface still seems to be a factor. But – and this is the key to the argument – game-by-game analysis across these same years indicates that playing on grass works against the Jays *only when their homer count is off*. When they are hitting homers, it does not seem to matter much what park they are playing in – natural-grass clubs do not appear to have a playing-surface advantage against them.

And so we are back at the notion that pennant contention in the A.L. East requires heavy lumber. (The club that wins the division nearly always also leads it and usually the league in homers.) This year, with Barfield often on the bench, Willie Aikens off his feed, and Willie Upshaw suffering a couple of brief but deep slumps, Jay power was off. George Bell could not make up the whole difference, and the club's h.r. total dropped about 15 per cent, from 167 to 143. So maybe it is not surprising the Jays did a little worse against the East this year.

Talk of Jay soft spots usually starts with the bullpen and moves to lefthanded pitching, and more strength in these areas would help. But if the Jays are ever to win the A.L. East, more power may be nearly as important.

Finally, and notably, the A.L. clubs which won their divisions this year were also the only two clubs in the league which played winning ball on both grass *and* turf surfaces: Detroit, a home grass club, played .638 ball on grass and .667 on turf; K.C., a home turf club, played .520 ball on turf and .516 on grass.

There are other questions, too. If Garth Iorg's slump continues, will Kelly Gruber come up? Gruber probably does need at least another full season in the minors.

Will Whitt and Buck Martinez be behind the plate again? Whitt, the Gentleman Jay, has been a constant presence this year. On offence he notched forty-six r.b.i.'s and fifteen homers in a little more than 300 at-bats, and on defence he was the club's anchor, hunkered down at his job in part or all of 120-odd games. He has not made a lot of news, but he has been as essential to the club as any of its headliners.

It is axiomatic that good pitching needs good catching, and at least some of the success of the Jays' starting staff must be credited to their receivers.

Will Cliff Johnson and Willie Aikens again be the d.h.'s? Aikens likely will be back; the assumption is he will return to his form of seasons past. But Johnson qualifies for free agency this season and will have to be re-signed. If he does go to another club, the Jays might solve their outfield dilemma by using the fourth outfielder as a d.h. – circulating the job among Bell, Barfield, and Collins. There is a lot to be said for having d.h.'s who are capable position players. It was the tactic the Tigers followed to good effect this year. A manager has more bench flexibility, and regulars have an occasional rest from their fielding job.

And maybe the most troublesome question of all: the pen. Ron Musselman may, these last few weeks, have pitched himself onto the staff for next year, Bryan Clark has likely pitched himself off it. Will Jim Gott and Jimmy Key stay in the pen? Dennis Lamp will be here, but in what role? And what about the main problem: will the club get a crack at a frontline stopper or somehow be able to manufacture one? And can they really hope to better their record without one?

A scad of uncertainties, too many to list, too early to guess at answers. Hot-stove season will come soon enough, time to think about the questions, argue them, puzzle with pieces. But one did watch the Jays in this final set with a bittersweet sense of time passing. Faces will change, old friends will go – gone with Bobby Bailor, Al Woods, Jesse Jefferson – and strangers will come in their place. Being a fan takes a tolerance for changes. Too, it takes patience.

The Jays went out their last day and got beat. They whacked a few balls into the teeth of the wind which, on another day, might have been gone. On this day they were just deep outs. Doyle Alexander, looking for his eighteenth win on only three days' rest, did not have the old magic. The result was an ignominious shutout, 4-0. Funny – the

Brewers could beat no one else in the league this year; against the others they played .385 ball. But the Jays, for them, were duck soup.

Jays vs. East Division Clubs, 1984

VS.	W	L
Baltimore	9	4
Boston	8	5
Cleveland	7	6
New York	5	8
Detroit	5	8
Milwaukee	3	10

The Jays still might have matched the Royals' eighth-season record if they had eked out this last game. But, for all that, only the Royals and the Miracle Mets played better eighth-season ball. All in all, it was a pretty good year. In

Expansion Club Records, Eighth Seasons

	W	L	PCT.	GB
New York Mets (1969)	100	62	.617	—
Kansas City Royals (1976)	90	72	.556	10
Toronto Blue Jays (1984)	89	73	.549	11
Houston Colt 45s/Astros (1969)	81	81	.500	19
Seattle Mariners (1984)	74	88	.457	26
San Diego Padres (1976)	73	89	.451	27
Los Angeles/California Angels (1968)	67	95	.414	33
Seattle Pilots/Milwaukee Brewers (1976)	66	95	.410	33½
Washington Senators/Texas Rangers (1968)	65	96	.404	34½
Montreal Expos (1976)	55	107	.340	45

spite of relative youth, for which the only resolution is time, in spite of a spate of mysterious and difficult slumps at key moments (one knows Clancy and Upshaw can have more consistent seasons) and in spite of a journeyman pen (on some days, greased lightning, but on others . . .), the Jays played better ball than twenty-one clubs* and survived the crunch of the A.L. East bested by only the remarkable Tigers, only the fourth club in major league history to lodge in first place for the duration of the season.

One wondered in that final game whether the Jays might do another of their ninth-inning cavalry charges and edge the Brewers for a last tense win, but it wasn't there. Milwaukee's young southpaw reliever Ray Searage had his stuff, and Bobby Cox's pinch-hitters didn't have theirs. Garth Iorg flied to right, Jesse Barfield popped to third. The last batter was Buck Martinez who flied to right too. That was all. The game was done, and baseball and the season were over.

But a season is never really over, not as long as anyone who was there is around to remember it, finger through the dusty stats (frozen now, like photographs) and give them life in recollection, replay the games and innings in the hot-stove league. The schedule does stop, but a season doesn't end. It lives on in the imagination's attic with all those other seasons carefully preserved since childhood. The 1955 Dodgers are still the Boys of Summer in the hot-stove league. Nellie Fox, Ernie Banks, Brooks Robinson are still in their prime. Tommy Agee and Ron Swoboda are still robbing Orioles of base hits in the Shea Stadium outfield. Bernie Carbo is still driving a fastball deep into Fenway's centrefield bleachers. Time doesn't exist here.

And season's end, anyway, is no place to stop a baseball book.

September 12, Toronto, Jays vs. Yanks. The evening air is a funny mix of summer and autumn, the breeze at one moment warm, at another laced with just enough chill to

---

* Besides the Tigers, the clubs who surpassed them were all in the N.L.: the Cubs (96-65), Padres (92-70), and Mets (90-72).

remind one that the summer game's days are numbered for this year. It is a Wednesday night, and the crowd in the bleachers is smallish.

On the mound for the Jays will be a young whipper-snapper, Doyle Alexander – whippersnapper, that is, measured against the hurler for the other side, name of Phil Niekro. And Alexander has trouble right from the start. Willie Randolph doubles, Bobby Meacham is hit by a pitch, and the next Yank batters are the A.L.'s leading hitters, Don Mattingly and Dave Winfield. But, oddly, one is not worried. There is something in the darkening twilight on which one cannot quite put one's finger, and one is sure Alexander will work out of the jam, the inning will turn out okay. And, sure enough, Mattingly pops up, Winfield whiffs, and even though Alexander loads the bases by plonking Don Baylor, his second hit batsman of the frame, one knows the Yanks will not score. Ken Griffey flies to left, and the side is retired.

Niekro takes the mound, and one watches carefully, attentively. It may be the last time we will see him pitch; he *has* to retire some day. The old man takes his time between pitches, walking down behind the mound, rubbing up the ball, taking off his cap and brushing a hand through what's left of his grey-white hair. He puts the cap back on and climbs back to the rubber and gazes in at the batter, some kid half his age with fire in belly and quick hands and cocky eyes. *Show me your stuff, old man. You ain't got it no more. What the hell's a relic like you doing out there anyway?*

Niekro has seemed almost weary until now – the long sojourn behind the mound, hike back up the hillock, patient study of yet one more tadpole with lumber in his hands. But now it's time to pitch, and suddenly there is spring in Niekro's step, easy grace in his fluid motion. The arm arcs, and a butterfly darts and bobs toward the plate. The young thumper gets big eyes and cocks his body. *Goddamn, I'm gonna knock this thing a country mile!* Swish. The lazy ball weaves around the bat and plops into the mitt of the catcher.

Nellie Fox was still playing ball when Niekro came up. The years were 1964 and 1965. Niekro was a rookie with the Milwaukee Braves. Fox, in his final seasons, was a Houston Colt .45. At one time or other they probably faced each other.

Niekro works Garcia and Collins for infield outs and retires Moseby on swinging strikes.

Alexander takes the mound again and gets in trouble again, allowing a leadoff single and then, with two out, another single. The next batter is Meacham, whom Alexander needs eleven pitches to retire – with the count full, Meacham fouls away five consecutive offerings. He finally pops to centre. In the frame's bottom Niekro once more rattles off the Jays one-two-three. His K victim this time is no kid but Cliff Johnson, who cuts hopelessly at Niekro's stuff. In the top of the third the Yanks also go one-two-three – not, however, without a bit of Jay luck. Winfield's bullet across the turf is aimed directly at Griffin, who would otherwise have had no play. And Baylor's drive to deep centre stays, barely, in the park for Moseby.

In the bottom of the third the Jays draw blood. Mulliniks pokes a knuckler for an *el cheapo* single – more Jay luck, really; it was a pretty good pitch, a vintage Niekro corkscrew. Mulliniks steals second, his first theft of the season, which he manages because of the time it takes for Niekro's stuff to reach the plate; it seems one has time to go out for a bag of nuts between Niekro's release and the ball's arrival home. Whitt moves Mulliniks to third with a fly to right, and Garcia pokes another one-penny single to drive the run home.

Alexander is in control now. The Yanks die quickly in the fourth, likewise the Jays, and the Yanks in the fifth. The Jays nibble out another run in the bottom of the fifth. Johnson singles – Niekro cannot, it seems, fool him twice – and Mulliniks moves him to second on a groundout. (Cox had Johnson running on the pitch, or the Yanks would have turned a d.p.) Whitt scores him with another chipped single.

Winfield fans to open the sixth, and Mulliniks now makes a marvelous play, grabbing a shot to his left off Baylor's bat and firing the peg to first for a split-second out, the kind of baseball that takes your breath away. Griffey grounds out, and the Jays come to bat. Moseby grounds out. Upshaw now is the first Jay to finally get all of one of Niekro's offerings – knucklers don't seem to bother Upshaw much; he can also hit Charlie Hough. The ball streaks deep into the right-centrefield gap, extra bases for sure. But at the base of the wall, Winfield, running like the wind, intercepts the ball before it comes to earth.

Abruptly we realize we are breathing rarefied air here. We had sensed it in the top of the first as Alexander worked out of trouble, again as we watched Niekro work and as the Jays scratched out their meagre runs. We sensed it more sharply still with Mulliniks' improbable play a moment earlier. Now with Winfield's stunning catch we understand: we had come to the park tonight mainly to see Phil Niekro's last hurrah and have stumbled instead, almost by accident, onto the trail of the perfect ballgame.

The Yanks go easily in the seventh, the Jays too. But Meacham leads off the eighth with a single to centre, and Don Mattingly lines a shot down the leftfield line – again, extra bases for sure. But somehow, incredibly, Dave Collins is there, plucks the ball from the air on a dead lateral run. Meacham, who was moving, must scramble back to first. He advances to third when Alexander errs on a pickoff attempt, throwing the ball past Upshaw where it ricochets down the rightfield line. Winfield singles Meacham home, and Bobby Cox comes to the mound. He talks to Alexander, listens, scratches the back of his head, and returns to the dugout. Alexander whiffs Baylor flailing (!) and retires Griffey on a pop to left.

With one out in the frame's bottom Collins lines a double, and now it is Yogi Berra's turn to visit the mound. He taps his left wrist, and Phil Niekro's night is done. He gives Berra the ball and, head bowed, returns slowly across the infield to the dugout. Dave Righetti comes in and strikes out

Moseby and Upshaw to retire the side. (They did not have a chance. After facing Niekro's slow stuff all night, they were suddenly confronted with Righetti's searing heat which cut them down like ducks in a shooting gallery – *ding! ding!*) The Yanks come to bat in the top of the ninth needing only a run to lock the score but do not get even a base runner. Alexander terminates them on quick infield outs – F6, F6, 4-3. The match is over.

And on the search for the perfect ballgame, it is another useful stop – *the game*, the way it was meant to be played and felt, its rhythms gentle, steady, taut, every pitch and every out a story, every play the tip of an iceberg of years of lore and memory. It was a game for the mantelpiece, a scorecard to tuck up there and forget and find by accident some long winter night when the windows are frosted and snow is swirling outside. The fielders will be arrayed under the lights again, and the batters will come to the plate to face the hard odds against them. The aging craftsmen on the mound will work slowly, carefully, caringly.

It did seem in the midst of that game, as Niekro loped down from the mound at inning's end and Alexander strode toward it, as the Yanks left the field and the Jays moved out to take their positions and toss warm-up balls and a batter stepped into the on-deck circle and swung a bat and knelt on one knee to wait patiently for Alexander to finish his practice throws – it did seem for just a special fleeting moment like maybe it would go on forever.

Final Standings, A.L. East

	W	L	PCT.	GB
Detroit	104	58	.642	—
Toronto	89	73	.549	15
New York	87	75	.537	17
Boston	86	76	.531	18
Baltimore	85	77	.525	19
Cleveland	75	87	.463	29
Milwaukee	67	94	.416	36½

Afterword

It is designed to break your heart. The game begins in the spring, when everything else begins again, and it blossoms in the summer, filling the afternoons and evenings, and then as soon as the chill rains come, it stops and leaves you to face the fall alone.
— A.B. Giamatti

Next year, though – now next year we gotta go for it.
— Lloyd Moseby

Epilogue

October 29
The Detroit Tigers hammered the Kansas City Royals three games to one to win the A.L. flag and blew the San Diego Padres out of the World Series four games to one. The Tigers were, for this season, destiny's team.

December 31
Cliff Johnson exercised his free agency and, in December, signed with the Texas Rangers. The Jays acquired journeyman slugger Jeff Burroughs to take Johnson's place as righty d.h.

Alfredo Griffin and Dave Collins left too, traded to Oakland in December for relief ace Bill Caudill. Interviewed after the trade, Griffin said he understood why the Jays had to make the move. And, he said, who knows, maybe some day he would be a Jay again.

February 7
Jim Gott also departed the Jays, traded in the midst of the snowy season to San Francisco for more bullpen strength, veteran Giant southpaw reliever Gary Lavelle.

And, finally, the bullpen in Cooperstown was notably strengthened this winter with the election, at last, of the fireman's fireman, Hoyt Wilhelm, to the Hall of Fame.

Appendix One:
Jays' Season Record, 1984

(Opponents in italic: road games. Pitchers in caps: starters.
Pitchers in italic: complete games.)

DATE OPP	SCORE	RECORD	POS/GB	W/L	GWRBI
Chapter 4					
4/4 SEA	L/2-3	0-1	T3/1	Lamp (0-1)	
4/5 SEA	W/13-5	1-1	T3/1	LEAL (1-0)	Griffin (1)
4/6 CAL	W/11-5	2-1	2/1	Key (1-0)	Upshaw (1)
4/7 CAL	W/3-1	3-1	3/1	STIEB (1-0)	Upshaw (2)
4/8 CAL	L/3-4	3-2	3/2	Jackson (0-1)	
4/9 OAK	L/3-4	3-3	T3/2½	Lamp (0-2)	
4/10 OAK	W/3-0	4-3	T2/2½	LEAL (2-0)	Barfield (1)
4/13 TEX	W/3-2	5-3	2/3	Lamp (1-2)	Collins (1)
4/14 TEX	L/2-6	5-4	T2/3½	CLANCY (0-1)	
4/15 TEX	W/2-1	6-4	2/3	Lamp (2-2)	Johnson (1)
Chapter 5					
4/17 BAL	W/3-2	7-4	2/2½	Key (2-0)	Bell (1)
4/18 BAL	W/7-1	8-4	2/2½	STIEB (2-0)	Collins (2)
4/19 BAL	W/2-1	9-4	2/1½	*CLANCY (1-1)*	Iorg (1)
4/20 CAL	L/6-10	9-5	2/2½	Acker (0-1)	
4/21 CAL	L/4-8	9-6	2/3½	GOTT (0-1)	
4/22 CAL	L/6-9	9-7	2/4½	Key (2-1)	
4/23 SEA	W/8-5	10-7	2/4	STIEB (3-0)	Moseby (1)
4/24 SEA	L/2-4	10-8	2/5½	CLANCY (1-2)	
4/25 OAK	W/11-0	11-8	2/5½	*LEAL (3-0)*	Bell (2)
4/26 OAK	L/4-7	11-9	3/6½	GOTT (0-2)	
4/27 KC	W/1-0	12-9	3/5½	ALEXANDER (1-0)	Bell (3)
4/28 KC	W/6-0	13-9	2/5½	*STIEB (4-0)*	Upshaw (3)
5/1 TEX	W/10-4	14-9	2/5½	LEAL (4-0)	Bell (4)
5/1 TEX	L/1-4	14-10	2/6½	ALEXANDER (1-1)	

DATE OPP	SCORE	RECORD	POS/GB	W/L	GWRBI
5/2 TEX	W/7-6	15-10	2/5½	CLANCY (2-2)	Upshaw (4)
5/4 KC	W/4-3	16-10	2/5	*STIEB (5-0)*	Griffin (2)
5/5 KC	W/10-1	17-10	2/5	GOTT (1-2)	Moseby (2)
5/6 KC	W/2-1	18-10	2/5	Jackson (1-1)	Johnson (2)
5/9 BAL	L/4-7	18-11	2/7	CLANCY (2-3)	
5/9 BAL	L/3-7	18-12	2/7½	Key (2-2)	
5/10 BAL	W/4-3	19-12	2/7	Jackson (2-1)	Upshaw (5)

Chapter 6

5/12 CLE	L/4-8	19-13	2/7½	Acker (0-2)	
5/15 MIN	W/5-2	20-13	2/8	Jackson (3-1)	Moseby (3)
5/16 MIN	W/8-7	21-13	2/8	ALEXANDER (2-1)	Leach (1)
5/17 CHI	W/3-2	22-13	2/7½	Jackson (4-1)	Moseby (4)
5/18 CHI	W/4-3	23-13	2/7½	CLANCY (3-3)	Collins (3)
5/19 CHI	W/1-0	24-13	2/7½	GOTT (2-2)	Collins (4)
5/20 CHI	L/0-3	24-14	2/8½	STIEB (5-1)	
5/21 MIN	W/3-2	25-14	2/8	*ALEXANDER (3-1)*	Collins (5)
5/22 MIN	W/3-2	26-14	2/8	Jackson (5-1)	Bell (5)
5/23 MIN	W/4-1	27-14	2/8	CLANCY (4-3)	Iorg (2)
5/25 CLE	W/5-1	28-14	2/7½	STIEB (6-1)	Bell (6)
5/26 CLE	W/2-1	29-14	2/6½	ALEXANDER (4-1)	Bell (7)
5/27 CLE	W/6-1	30-14	2/5½	*LEAL (5-0)*	Aikens (1)
5/27 CLE	W/6-5	31-14	2/5	Jackson (6-1)	Fernandez (1)
5/29 CHI	L/1-8	31-15	2/5½	CLANCY (4-4)	
5/30 CHI	W/2-1	32-15	2/5½	STIEB (7-1)	Martinez (1)
6/1 NY	W/10-2	33-15	2/5½	ALEXANDER (5-1)	Barfield (2)
6/2 NY	W/9-8	34-15	2/4½	Lamp (3-2)	Whitt (1)
6/3 NY	L/2-15	34-16	2/4½	CLANCY (4-5)	

Chapter 7

6/4 DET	L/3-6	34-17	2/5½	Key (2-3)	
6/5 DET	W/8-4	35-17	2/4½	Acker (1-2)	Aikens (2)
6/6 DET	W/6-3	36-17	2/3½	LEAL (6-0)	None
6/7 DET	L/3-5	36-18	2/4½	CLANCY (4-6)	
6/8 NY	L/3-4	36-19	2/5½	Acker (1-3)	
6/9 NY	L/1-2	36-20	2/5½	*STIEB (7-2)*	
6/10 NY	L/3-5	36-21	2/7	ALEXANDER (5-2)	
6/11 DET	L/4-5	36-22	2/8	LEAL (6-1)	
6/12 DET	W/12-3	37-22	2/7	CLANCY (5 6)	Collins (6)
6/13 DET	W/7-3	38-22	2/6	STIEB (8-2)	Mulliniks (1)

Chapter 8

DATE OPP	SCORE	RECORD	POS/GB	W/L	GWRBI
6/15 BOS	W/4-3	39-22	2/6	Lamp (4-2)	Mulliniks (2)
6/16 BOS	W/7-0	40-22	2/6	*LEAL (7-1)*	Moseby (5)
6/17 BOS	W/5-3	41-22	2/6	CLANCY (6-6)	Mulliniks (3)
6/19 MIL	L/5-6	41-23	2/6½	Key (2-4)	
6/20 MIL	L/4-5	41-24	2/7½	ALEXANDER (5-3)	
6/21 BOS	W/5-2	42-24	2/6½	*LEAL (8-1)*	Upshaw (6)
6/22 BOS	L/1-8	42-25	2/7½	CLANCY (6-7)	
6/23 BOS	W/9-3	43-25	2/7½	GOTT (3-2)	Moseby (6)
6/24 BOS	L/3-5	43-26	2/8½	Lamp (4-3)	
6/25 MIL	L/1-2	43-27	2/8½	ALEXANDER (5-4)	
6/25 MIL	L/4-9	43-28	2/9	ACKER (1-4)	
6/26 MIL	L/3-6	43-29	2/10	LEAL (8-2)	
6/27 MIL	L/1-5	43-30	2/10	CLANCY (6-8)	
6/28 OAK	W/9-6	44-30	2/9½	GOTT (4-2)	Garcia (1)
6/29 OAK	L/1-2	44-31	2/10	*STIEB (8-3)*	
6/30 OAK	W/6-1	45-31	2/10	*ALEXANDER (6-4)*	Johnson (3)
7/1 OAK	W/7-6	46-31	2/9	Acker (2-4)	Barfield (3)
7/2 CAL	L/3-6	46-32	2/9	CLANCY (6-9)	
7/3 CAL	W/4-0	47-32	2/8	*GOTT (5-2)*	Garcia (2)
7/4 CAL	W/6-3	48-32	2/7	STIEB (9-3)	Whitt (2)
7/5 SEA	W/10-8	49-32	2/7	ALEXANDER (7-4)	Upshaw (7)
7/6 SEA	W/9-2	50-32	2/6	*LEAL (9-2)*	Iorg (3)
7/7 SEA	L/4-8	50-33	2/7	CLANCY (6-10)	
7/8 SEA	L/1-7	50-34	2/7	GOTT (5-3)	

Chapter 9

DATE OPP	SCORE	RECORD	POS/GB	W/L	GWRBI
7/12 OAK	L/4-7	50-35	2/7	Lamp (4-4)	
7/13 OAK	W/6-3	51-35	2/7	LEAL (10-2)	Mulliniks (4)
7/14 OAK	W/2-1	52-35	2/7	*STIEB (10-3)*	Collins (7)
7/15 OAK	W/6-3	53-35	2/7	CLANCY (7-10)	Garcia (3)
7/16 CAL	L/0-3	53-36	2/8	GOTT (5-4)	
7/17 CAL	L/3-5	53-37	2/9	Acker (2-5)	
7/18 CAL	W/8-2	54-37	2/8	*LEAL (11-2)*	Upshaw (8)
7/19 SEA	W/8-1	55-37	2/8	STIEB (11-3)	None
7/20 SEA	W/12-7	56-37	2/8	Acker (3-5)	Fernandez (2)
7/21 SEA	L/3-9	56-38	2/9	Lamp (4-5)	
7/22 SEA	W/5-3	57-38	2/9	ALEXANDER (8-4)	Johnson (4)
7/23 KC	L/8-9	57-39	2/10	Jackson (6-2)	
7/23 KC	L/2-7	57-40	2/10½	GOTT (5-5)	
7/24 KC	L/4-5	57-41	2/11½	STIEB (11-4)	
7/25 KC	L/4-5	57-42	2/11½	Clark (0-1)	

Chapter 10

DATE OPP	SCORE	RECORD	POS/GB	W/L	GWRBI
7/27 TEX	L/2-4	57-43	2/12	*ALEXANDER (8-5)*	
7/28 TEX	L/4-5	57-44	2/12	Jackson (6-3)	
7/29 TEX	W/6-2	58-44	2/12	*STIEB (12-4)*	Mulliniks (5)
7/30 KC	L/4-7	58-45	2/12½	*CLANCY (7-11)*	
7/31 KC	W/6-5	59-45	2/12	*ALEXANDER (9-5)*	Upshaw (9)
8/1 KC	W/4-1	60-45	2/11	*LEAL (12-2)*	Garcia (4)
8/3 BAL	W/5-2	61-45	2/10½	*Jackson (7-3)*	Martinez (2)
8/4 BAL	W/6-2	62-45	2/9½	*CLANCY (8-11)*	Johnson (5)
8/5 BAL	W/4-3	63-45	2/8	Key (3-4)	Johnson (6)
8/6 TEX	L/4-5	63-46	2/8½	Jackson (7-4)	
8/7 TEX	L/6-7	63-47	2/9	Lamp (4-6)	
8/8 TEX	W/7-2	64-47	2/8	CLANCY (9-11)	Collins (8)

Chapter 11

DATE OPP	SCORE	RECORD	POS/GB	W/L	GWRBI
8/10 BAL	W/2-0	65-47	2/8	*ALEXANDER (10-5)*	Fernandez (3)
8/11 BAL	W/3-2	66-47	2/8	*Gott (6-5)*	Bell (8)
8/12 BAL	L/4-5	66-48	2/9	*Jackson (7-5)*	
8/13 BAL	L/1-2	66-49	2/9½	*CLANCY (9-12)*	
8/14 CLE	W/8-1	67-49	2/8½	ALEXANDER (11-5)	Garcia (5)
8-14 CLE	W/9-5	68-49	2/7½	Lamp (5-6)	Bell (9)
8/15 CLE	L/1-16	68-50	2/8½	LEAL (12-3)	
8/15 CLE	L/3-4	68-51	2/9	Key (3-5)	
8/16 CLE	L/5-6	68-52	2/10	Lamp (5-7)	
8/17 CHI	W/4-3	69-52	2/10	*CLANCY (10-12)*	Whitt (3)
8/18 CHI	L/6-7	69-53	2/11	Jackson (7-6)	
8/19 CHI	W/7-4	70-53	2/10	Key (4-5)	Collins (9)
8/21 CLE	L/1-3	70-54	2/11½	STIEB (12-5)	
8/22 CLE	L/3-13	70-55	2/12½	CLANCY (10-13)	
8-23 CLE	W/6-1	71-55	2/12	*ALEXANDER (12-5)*	Whitt (4)
8/24 MIN	W/6-2	72-55	2/11	LEAL (13-3)	Johnson (7)
8/25 MIN	L/4-5	72-56	2/12	Gott (6-6)	
8/26 MIN	W/2-1	73-56	2/12	*STIEB (13-5)*	Whitt (5)
8/27 MIN	W/5-2	74-56	2/11½	LAMP (6-7)	None
8/28 CHI	W/7-6	75-56	2/11½	Clark (1-1)	Garcia (6)
8/29 CHI	L/5-8	75-57	2/11½	LEAL (13-4)	
8/30 CHI	W/4-3	76-57	2/10½	Gott (7-6)	Moseby (7)
8/31 MIN	W/7-0	77-57	2/10½	*STIEB (14-5)*	Collins (10)
9/1 MIN	W/12-4	78-57	2/9½	LAMP (7-7)	Garcia (7)
9/2 MIN	W/6-0	79-57	2/8½	*ALEXANDER (13-5)*	Bell (10)

DATE OPP	SCORE	RECORD	POS/GB	W/L	GWRBI

Chapter 12

DATE OPP	SCORE	RECORD	POS/GB	W/L	GWRBI
9/3 NY	L/0-2	79-58	2/8½	LEAL (13-5)	
9/4 NY	W/6-4	80-58	2/7½	CLANCY (11-13)	Bell (1)
9/5 NY	L/4-3	80-59	2/8½	Jackson (7-7)	
9/7 DET	L/4-7	80-60	2/9½	Musselman (0-1)	
9/8 DET	L/4-10	80-61	2/10½	LEAL (13-6)	
9/9 DET	L/2-7	80-62	2/11½	CLANCY (11-14)	
9/10 NY	L/2-6	80-63	2/11½	STIEB (14-6)	
9/11 NY	W/10-3	81-63	2/11½	LAMP (8-7)	Martinez (3)
9/12 NY	W/2-1	82-63	2/10½	*ALEXANDER (14-5)*	Garcia (8)
9/13 NY	L/1-6	82-64	2/11	LEAL (13-7)	
9/14 DET	W/7-2	83-64	2/10	CLANCY (12-14)	Aikens (3)
9/15 DET	L/1-2	83-65	2/11	*STIEB (14-7)*	
9/16 DET	L/3-8	83-66	2/12	CLARK (1-2)	
9/17 BOS	W/5-4	84-66	2/12	*ALEXANDER (15-5)*	Iorg (4)
9/18 BOS	L/3-10	84-67	2/13	LEAL (13-8)	
9/19 BOS	L/4-10	84-68	2/14	CLANCY (12-15)	
9/20 MIL	W/6-4	85-68	2/13½	STIEB (15-7)	Collins (11)
9/21 MIL	L/1-5	85-69	2/13½	LAMP (8-8)	
9/22 MIL	W/2-1	86-69	2/13½	*ALEXANDER (16-5)*	Mulliniks (6)
9/23 MIL	L/5-8	86-70	2/14½	Jackson (7-8)	
9/24 BOS	W/9-8	87-70	2/14½	CLANCY (13-15)	Moseby (8)
9/25 BOS	L/6-14	87-71	2/15½	STIEB (15-8)	
9/26 BOS	W/8-4	88-71	2/14½	*ALEXANDER (17-5)*	Whitt (6)

Chapter 13

DATE OPP	SCORE	RECORD	POS/GB	W/L	GWRBI
9/28 MIL	L/3-4	88-72	2/15	Musselman (0-2)	
9/29 MIL	W/5-4	89-72	2/15	*STIEB (16-8)*	Manrique (1)
9/30 MIL	L/0-4	89-73	2/15	*ALEXANDER (17-6)*	

Appendix Two: Stats

Final Standings, American League

	W	L	PCT.	GB
Detroit	104	58	.642	—
Toronto	89	73	.549	15
New York	87	75	.537	17
Boston	86	76	.531	18
Baltimore	85	77	.525	19
Kansas City	84	78	.519	20
Minnesota	81	81	.500	23
California	81	81	.500	23
Oakland	77	85	.475	27
Cleveland	75	87	.463	29
Seattle	74	88	.457	30
Chicago	74	88	.457	30
Texas	69	92	.429	34½
Milwaukee	67	94	.416	36½

Blue Jays' Club Stats, 1984

Club Won/Lost Records

	JAYS	RANK	A.L. AVG.	RANKED FIRST	RANKED LAST
vs. RHP	.509	6th	.497	.673 (DET)	.410 (TEX)
	57-55			68-33	48-69
vs. LHP	.640	1st	.506		.376 (MIL)
	32-18				19-30
Home	.605	3rd	.537	.646 (DET)	.425 (TEX)
	49-32			53-29	34-46
Road	.494	5th	.463	.638 (DET)	.363 (MIL)
	40-41			51-29	29-51
Ex.-Inn. Games	.333	13th	.500	.846 (DET)	.231 (CHI)
	6-12			11-2	3-10
One-Run Games	.576	3rd	.500	.694 (DET)	.347 (CHI)
	34-25			25-11	17-32
Two-Run Games	.467	10th	.500	.611 (BAL)	.292 (SEA)
	7-8			22-14	7-17
Grass	.460	10th	.500	.638 (DET)	.416 (MIL)
	29-34			88-50	57-80
Turf	.606	2nd	.500	.667 (DET)	.333 (BOS)
	60-39			16-8	8-16
vs. East	.474	7th	.477	.602 (DET)	.385 (CLEV)
	37-41			47-31	30-48
vs. West	.619	2nd	.523	.678 (DET)	.422 (MIL)
	52-32			57-27	35-48
Shutouts Lost	4	1st	9		13 (NY, KC)

Club Batting

	JAYS	RANK	A.L. AVG.	RANKED FIRST	RANKED LAST
Batting Avg.	.273	3rd	.264	.283 (BOS)	.247 (CHI)
Runs	750	5th	716	829 (DET)	641 (MIL
Hits	1555	3rd	1467	1598 (BOS)	1360 (CHI)
Total Bases	2395	3rd	2214	2490 (BOS)	2038 (MIL)
2Bs	275	2nd	246	276 (NY)	211 (CAL)
3Bs	68	1st	38		23 (BAL)
HRs	143	7th	141	187 (DET)	96 (MIL)
RBIs	702	5th	675	787 (DET)	598 (MIL)
SHs	35	13th	45	66 (SEA)	26 (MIN)
SFs	49	6th	51	77 (OAK)	38 (SEA)
HBs	52	1st	30		20 (BOS, TEX)
BBs	460	10th	512	620 (BAL)	400 (KC)
SOs	815	5th	826	673 (NY, MIL)	941 (DET)
SBs	193	1st	93		37 (BOS)
GIDPs	89	1st	125		152 (MIL)
LOBs	1177	7th	1142	1071 (KC)	1217 (NY)
Slugging Pct.	.421	3rd	.398	.441 (BOS)	.370 (MIL)
On-Base Pct.	.331	5th	.326	.342 (DET)	.313 (TEX)
DH Bat. Avg.	.270	4th	.256	.306 (BOS)	.219 (BAL)
DH Slg. Pct.	.458	3rd	.418	.515 (BOS)	.311 (BAL)
DH OB Pct.	.356	2nd	.330	.362 (BOS)	.292 (MIL)
PH At-Bats	215	1st	148		89 (MIL)
PH Bat. Avg.	.284	2nd	.245	.312 (DET)	.174 (OAK)
PH Slg. Pct.	.433	4th	.362	.489 (DET)	.246 (CLE)
PH OB Pct.	.368	2nd	.324	.394 (DET)	.250 (OAK)

Club Pitching

	JAYS	RANK	A.L. AVG.	RANKED FIRST	RANKED LAST
ERA	3.87	5th	3.99	3.49 (DET)	4.49 (OAK)
CGs	34	6th	28	48 (BAL)	13 (MIL)
Shutouts	10	5th	9	13 (BAL)	4 (SEA)
Saves	33	9th	37	51 (DET)	21 (TEX)
Hits	1433	6th	1467	1358 (DET)	1554 (OAK)
HRs	140	7th	141	120 (NY)	159 (MIN)
HBs	34	9th	30	20 (NY)	40 (SEA)
Uninten. BBs	484	10th	472	413 (MIN, KC)	566 (SEA)
SOs	875	5th	826	992 (NY)	695 (OAK)
WPs	41	6th	44	31 (KC)	61 (TEX)
BKs	2	1st	7		11 (CLE, SEA)

Club Fielding

	JAYS	RANK	A.L. AVG.	RANKED FIRST	RANKED LAST
Fielding Avg.	.980	4th	.979	.981 (BAL)	.975 (OAK)
DPs	166	4th	155	175 (NY)	127 (BOS)
PBs	9	7th	10	3 (KC)	32 (TEX)

Blue Jays' Batting Stats, 1984

	AVG	G	AB	R	H	2B	3B	HR	RBI	SH	SF	HB	BB	SO	SB	CS	SLG	OBP
Aikens	.205	93	234	21	48	7	0	11	26	0	0	2	29	56	0	0	.376	.298
Barfield	.285	110	320	51	91	14	1	14	49	1	2	2	35	81	8	2	.466	.357
Bell	.292	159	606	85	177	39	4	26	87	0	3	8	24	86	11	2	.498	.326
Collins	.308	128	441	59	136	24	15	2	44	6	3	9	33	41	60	14	.444	.366
Fernandez	.270	88	233	29	63	5	3	3	19	2	2	0	17	15	5	7	.356	.317
Garcia	.284	152	633	79	180	32	5	5	46	3	4	9	16	46	46	12	.374	.310
Griffin	.241	140	419	53	101	8	2	4	30	13	4	1	4	33	11	3	.298	.248
Gruber	.063	15	16	1	1	0	0	1	2	0	0	0	0	5	0	0	.250	.063
Hernandez	.500	3	2	1	1	0	0	0	0	0	0	0	0	0	0	0	.500	.500
Iorg	.227	121	247	24	56	10	3	1	25	3	1	1	5	16	1	3	.304	.244
Johnson	.304	127	359	51	109	23	1	16	61	0	3	3	50	62	0	1	.507	.390
Leach	.261	65	88	11	23	6	2	0	7	0	1	0	8	14	0	0	.375	.320
Marrique	.333	10	9	0	3	0	0	0	1	0	0	0	0	1	0	0	.333	.333
Martinez	.220	102	232	24	51	13	1	5	37	1	9	2	29	49	0	3	.349	.301
Moseby	.280	158	592	97	166	28	15	18	92	3	7	8	78	122	39	9	.470	.368
Mulliniks	.324	125	343	41	111	21	5	3	42	0	2	1	33	44	2	3	.440	.383
Petralli	.000	3	3	0	0	0	0	0	0	0	0	0	0	0	0	0	.000	.000
Shepherd	.000	12	4	0	0	0	0	0	0	0	0	0	0	3	0	1	.000	.000
Upshaw	.278	152	569	79	158	31	9	19	84	3	3	5	55	86	10	4	.464	.345
Webster	.227	26	22	9	5	2	1	0	4	0	0	0	1	7	0	0	.409	.261
Whitt	.238	124	315	35	75	12	1	15	46	0	5	1	43	48	0	3	.425	.327

Blue Jays' Pitching Stats, 1984

	W	L	PCT	ERA	G	GS	CG	SHO	SV	INNP	H	R	ER	HR	HB	BB	SO	WP
Acker	3	5	.375	4.38	32	3	0	0	1	72.0	79	39	35	3	6	25	33	5
Alexander	17	6	.739	3.13	36	35	11	2	0	261.2	238	99	91	21	3	59	139	2
Clancy	13	15	.464	5.12	36	36	5	0	0	219.2	249	132	125	25	3	88	118	10
Clark	1	2	.333	5.91	20	3	0	0	0	45.2	66	33	30	6	1	22	21	6
Gott	7	6	.538	4.02	35	12	1	1	2	109.2	93	54	49	7	3	49	73	1
Jackson	7	8	.467	3.56	54	0	0	0	10	86.0	73	40	34	12	1	31	58	4
Key	4	5	.444	4.65	63	0	0	0	10	62.0	70	37	32	8	1	32	44	3
Lamp	8	8	.500	4.55	56	4	0	0	9	85.0	97	53	43	9	1	38	45	2
Leach	0	0	.000	27.00	1	0	0	0	0	1.0	2	3	3	1	0	2	0	0
Leal	13	8	.619	3.89	35	35	6	2	0	222.1	221	106	96	27	4	77	134	5
McLaughlin	0	0	.000	2.53	6	0	0	0	0	10.2	12	6	3	0	0	7	3	1
Musselman	0	2	.000	2.11	11	0	0	0	1	21.1	18	7	5	2	0	10	9	0
Stieb	16	8	.667	2.83	35	35	11	2	0	267.0	215	87	84	19	11	88	198	2

Acknowledgements

Thanks to Ellen Murray, Brian Cranley, Charis Wahl, and Marian Hebb; and thanks, too, to Howard Starkman, Judy Van Zutphen, and Gary Oswald.

Printed in Canada

g

HERE AT LAST IS THE ULTIMATE BOOK FOR THE SERIOUS BLUE JAYS FAN

(If you need the linescores more than
a cup of coffee in the morning, you qualify.)

A baseball season is never really over. Long after the final out,
fans relive the glories and groans of the past season. *JAYS!* is
the story of the Toronto Blue Jays' dramatic 1984 season. The
book brings alive again the marvelous pitching performances
of Dave Stieb and Doyle Alexander; Alfredo Griffin and
Tony Fernandez's intense rivalry for the shortstop position;
Dave Collins' relentless tenacity at the plate and on the
basepaths; the emergence of George Bell as a potential
superstar; and the exasperating, snatching-defeat-from-the-
jaws-of-victory performance of the team's bullpen.
But mostly *JAYS!* is about baseball, about the game and its
pleasures and the countless small moments of tension and
drama that shape the texture of a season. Included are a folio
of photographs and enough stats to keep a fan happy through
the lengthiest rain delay.

Jon Caulfield is a baseball fan who alternates residence
between west-end Toronto and the Country of Baseball.

Cover Design: Tad Aronowicz
Cover photo courtesy of the Toronto Blue Jays

McClelland and Stewart Limited
The Canadian Publishers